The Influenza Pandemic of 1918

The Influenza Pandemic of 1918

Virginia Aronson

CHELSEA HOUSE PUBLISHERS
Philadelphia

CHELSEA HOUSE PUBLISHERS

Editor in Chief Stephen Reginald
Production Manager Pamela Loos
Art Director Sara Davis
Director of Photography Judy L. Hasday
Managing Editor James D. Gallagher
Senior Production Editor J. Christopher Higgins

Staff for THE INFLUENZA PANDEMIC OF 1918

Senior Editor John Ziff
Editorial Assistant Rob Quinn
Associate Art Director Takeshi Takahashi
Picture Researcher Patricia Burns
Designer Keith Trego
Cover Illustrator Sara Davis

First Printing

1 3 5 7 9 8 6 4 2

The Chelsea House World Wide Web address is
http://www.chelseahouse.com

Library of Congress Cataloging-in-Publication Data

Aronson, Virginia.
The influenza pandemic of 1918 / Virginia Aronson.
    p. cm. — (Great disasters: reforms and ramifications)
Includes bibliographical references and index.
Summary: Discusses the outbreak and worldwide spread of the deadly Spanish flu in 1918, methods of treating it, and efforts to study this killer virus and others like it.

ISBN 0-7910-5263-X

1. Influenza—History—Juvenile literature. [1. Influenza—History. 2. Epidemics.] I. Title. II. Series.
RC150.4.A76 2000
614.5'18'09041—dc21   00-022390

Contents

GREAT DISASTERS
REFORMS and RAMIFICATIONS

Jill McCaffrey
National Chairman
Armed Forces Emergency Services
American Red Cross

Introduction

isasters have always been a source of fascination and awe. Tales of a great flood that nearly wipes out all life are among humanity's oldest recorded stories, dating at least from the second millennium B.C., and they appear in cultures from the Middle East to the Arctic Circle to the southernmost tip of South America and the islands of Polynesia. Typically gods are at the center of these ancient disaster tales—which is perhaps not too surprising, given the fact that the tales originated during a time when human beings were at the mercy of natural forces they did not understand.

To a great extent, we still are at the mercy of nature, as anyone who reads the newspapers or watches nightly news broadcasts can attest. Hurricanes, earthquakes, tornados, wildfires, and floods continue to exact a heavy toll in suffering and death, despite our considerable knowledge of the workings of the physical world. If science has offered only limited protection from the consequences of natural disasters, it has in no way diminished our fascination with them. Perhaps that's because the scale and power of natural disasters force us as individuals to confront our relatively insignificant place in the physical world and remind us of the fragility and transience of our lives. Perhaps it's because we can imagine ourselves in the midst of dire circumstances and wonder how we would respond. Perhaps it's because disasters seem to bring out the best and worst instincts of humanity: altruism and selfishness, courage and cowardice, generosity and greed.

As one of the national chairmen of the American Red Cross, a humanitarian organization that provides relief for victims of disasters, I have had the privilege of seeing some of humanity's best instincts. I have witnessed communities pulling together in the face of trauma; I have seen thousands of people answer the call to help total strangers in their time of need.

Of course, helping victims after a tragedy is not the only way, or even the best way, to deal with disaster. In many cases planning and preparation can minimize damage and loss of life—or even avoid a disaster entirely. For, as history repeatedly shows, many disasters are caused not by nature but by human folly, shortsightedness, and unethical conduct. For example, when a land developer wanted to create a lake for his exclusive resort club in Pennsylvania's Allegheny Mountains in 1880, he ignored expert warnings and cut corners in reconstructing an earthen dam. On May 31, 1889, the dam gave way, unleashing 20 million tons of water on the towns below. The Johnstown Flood, the deadliest in American history, claimed more than 2,200 lives. Greed and negligence would figure prominently in the Triangle Shirtwaist Company fire in 1911. Deplorable conditions in the garment sweatshop, along with a failure to give any thought to the safety of workers, led to the tragic deaths of 146 persons. Technology outstripped wisdom only a year later, when the designers of the luxury liner *Titanic* smugly declared their state-of-the-art ship "unsinkable," seeing no need to provide lifeboat capacity for everyone onboard. On the night of April 14, 1912, more than 1,500 passengers and crew paid for this hubris with their lives after the ship collided with an iceberg and sank. But human catastrophes aren't always the unforeseen consequences of carelessness or folly. In the 1940s the leaders of Nazi Germany purposefully and systematically set out to exterminate all Jews, along with Gypsies, homosexuals, the mentally ill, and other so-called undesirables. More recently terrorists have targeted random members of society, blowing up airplanes and buildings in an effort to advance their political agendas.

The books in the GREAT DISASTERS: REFORMS AND RAMIFICATIONS series examine these and other famous disasters, natural and human made. They explain the causes of the disasters, describe in detail how events unfolded, and paint vivid portraits of the people caught up in dangerous circumstances. But these books are more than just accounts of what happened to whom and why. For they place the disasters in historical perspective, showing how people's attitudes and actions changed and detailing the steps society took in the wake of each calamity. And in the end, the most important lesson we can learn from any disaster—as well as the most fitting tribute to those who suffered and died—is how to avoid a repeat in the future.

In Search
of a Killer

Six crosses and a head-stone mark the graves of seven miners who died in 1918 in the Norwegian village of Longyearbyen, in the far-north Svalbard island group. Eighty years after the miners' deaths, scientists hoped that exhuming their bodies would yield important clues about the virus that caused one of the dead-liest disease outbreaks in history.

In June 1951, the Alaskan coastal village of Brevig Mission, located just 75 miles south of the Arctic Circle, witnessed an unusual scene. After setting a series of small fires to warm up the permafrost—ground so cold it never completely thaws—a visitor from Iowa began digging in the village cemetery. The visitor, Johan V. Hultin, was on the trail of a killer. This was no ordinary killer, however: it had slaughtered as many as 40 million people.

The killer was a flu virus that came to be known as the Spanish influenza. Striking between 1918 and early 1919, it became the deadliest plague since the Middle Ages, when the Black Death wiped out one-third of Europe's population and ravaged Asia and parts of North

Africa over the course of several years. The Spanish influenza, by contrast, was truly worldwide in its devastation and extremely quick in its onset. In less than a year, the flu claimed more innocent victims faster than any disaster in recorded history. No war, no famine, no infection had ever proved so lethal for so many in such a short period of time.

Unlike most flu viruses—which are mild, posing a serious threat only to elderly people, children, and those with weakened immune systems—the Spanish influenza devastated healthy young individuals. Pregnant women typically died, and the flu proved fatal to nearly as many fit American soldiers as did World War I, which was being waged when the disease struck. In fact, the deadly flu killed more Americans than World War I, World War II, the Korean War, and the Vietnam War *combined*. By the time the flu had swept across the globe in three furious waves, it had killed an estimated 1 in every 100 people *in the entire world*.

Obviously, the 1918 Spanish influenza was not just any flu. It was a pandemic—that is, a disease occurring in large numbers in many areas of the world simultaneously. And it was caused by something unknown to the doctors and scientists of the time: a virus.

In the United States, between 600,000 and 700,000 citizens died during the 1918 pandemic. This was equivalent to 2 percent of the American population, killed off in less than a year. In Philadelphia alone, more than 7,500 people died in a single two-week period, their bodies stacked inside chaotic city morgues in piles three and four deep.

Eighty years later, the terrifying death toll of the Spanish influenza had been forgotten by most of the

world. Then, in 1998, dedicated scientists finally identified the killer virus's genetic code—the sequence of
genes that determine the specific physical characteris-
tics of all living organisms.

In 1918, however, there were no electron micro-
scopes, the special high-powered equipment used for
viewing the tiniest microorganisms. Living things as
small as viruses were as yet undiscovered. But ever
since the Spanish flu ripped across the planet, leaving
millions of people weak or dead, scientists and medical
researchers have believed that, if the killer could be
identified and analyzed, a vaccine might be developed
to protect the world from a future pandemic. Finally,
the Spanish influenza vaccine has become a public
health reality, rather than the lifelong dream of idealis-
tic researchers—like Dr. Johan V. Hultin, the young
man who dug up the cemetery of Brevig Mission,
Alaska, in June 1951.

In 1949, Dr. Hultin was a medical student studying
virology, the science of diseases caused by viruses. On
sabbatical from his native Sweden, he was pursuing his
studies at the University of Iowa when a professor
informed him that next to nothing had been discovered
about the Spanish influenza virus. At that time, scientists had still not been able to examine the actual virus
because, it was believed, no one had preserved tissue or
blood specimens from the victims back in 1918. But,
Hultin's professor told him, there was one way a sample of the virus could be found: a scientist could travel
to the far north, where the bodies of flu victims buried
in 1918 might still be frozen in the permafrost. Within
these frozen corpses there might be some living virus
lying dormant in the victims' body tissues.

Dr. Hultin was intrigued. He loved to travel, he enjoyed adventure, and he knew the topic would be perfect for a research paper. He began to review scores of death records from Alaska, trying to pinpoint a native village that had experienced an abnormally high death rate in 1918, which might indicate an influenza outbreak. The Spanish influenza, also known as the Spanish Lady, had spared few places in the world. As isolated and sparsely populated as it was early in the 20th century, Alaska had been hit hard by the deadly Lady. The native Indians, Aleuts, and Eskimos had died in greater percentages than any other peoples in the American empire.

After securing a grant from his university, Dr. Hultin traveled to Brevig Mission. During one calamitous week in 1918, the isolated mission had seen 72 citizens die—and the original population of the tiny village had totaled only 80. Dr. Hultin felt certain that the Spanish Lady had done her deadly dance in Brevig Mission.

On a bleak day in June 1951, Dr. Hultin met with Brevig Mission's tribal elders, explaining to the local council what he wished to do. Through a translator, they agreed to allow the visitor to dig up the old burial ground.

The temperature was mild, in the 40s and 50s, but Dr. Hultin had to thaw out the earth in the cemetery before he could begin to dig. So he built small fires across the frozen ground. After two days of digging in the treeless tundra, he unearthed a body from the mass grave: a little girl of age 10 or so, her black hair braided, her skin well preserved.

Samples of the girl's lungs were removed. This

particular tissue was selected because the Spanish influenza was a respiratory tract disease that most brutally attacked the lungs. Dr. Hultin brought the girl's lung tissue back to his lab in Iowa, where he carefully sliced it up. For the next six weeks, he attempted to culture the virus that he hoped remained in the lung tissue, trying to induce it to grow in lab animals and in a special medium. Nothing happened. Another group of researchers used Dr. Hultin's samples in a separate study, but that group also failed to culture the virus.

Dr. Hultin wrote a research paper on his efforts. He went on to complete his medical training, becoming a pathologist, a doctor who specializes in the analysis and

Researcher Kirsty Duncan and an associate use ground-penetrating radar to image the bodies of the Longyearbyen miners, October 1997. After determining that the bodies were still frozen, Duncan and her international team of pathologists, virologists, and excavation experts made arrangements to exhume and autopsy them in 1998.

identification of diseases. He got married, raised a family, and settled in the San Francisco area. He climbed mountains, sailed, and autopsied dead bodies for more than four and a half decades. All this time, though, he never let go of his dream: to track down the killer virus of 1918, the elusive Spanish Lady.

Dr. Hultin wasn't the only scientist with dreams of saving the world from a return visit of the deadliest virus in history. In the 1990s, Kirsty Duncan, a young medical geographer and climatologist from Canada, was studying diseases and their incidence in various locations and environments when she first read about the Spanish influenza of 1918. "I was absolutely fascinated—horrified, more than anything—that we didn't know what caused this disease," she told a journalist in 1997. "I said to my husband, 'I'm going to find the cause of the Spanish flu.'"

As Dr. Hultin had done decades before her, Kirsty Duncan began to review Alaskan death certificates from 1918. "I found all kinds of cases of Spanish flu. The problem was trying to decipher where the permafrost was," she later explained.

She decided to focus on Norway instead when a friend returned from the northern European country and mentioned the permafrost there. Duncan then researched the impact of the Spanish influenza on Svalbard, the huge group of islands located about 600 miles north of Norway. Her focus eventually narrowed on Longyearbyen, Svalbard's major port. An isolated settlement and former coal-mining town, Longyearbyen is less than 800 miles from the North Pole. It's a chilly little village of around 1,000 people.

At Duncan's request, a schoolteacher in Longyear-

Biohazard suits, a containment tent (seen in the background), and special autopsy techniques were among the precautions the Duncan team used to prevent the accidental release of potentially deadly virus. Still, a prominent biologist called the expedition "one of the most dangerous things people have ever done."

byen examined some old coal-company diaries and found a record of the deaths of seven young miners in 1918 from Spanish influenza. Duncan next contacted the minister at the church in Longyearbyen to ask if there were marked graves in the town cemetery for these seven young men. The minister confirmed the existence of the grave sites, and Duncan got ready to travel.

The governor of Svalbard secured approval for Duncan's investigation from all the necessary people—the Norwegian medical research community, the church in Longyearbyen, the town council, and the seven victims' living descendants. In May of 1997, Duncan flew to Longyearbyen, where she walked up the gravel road from the town church to the ice-covered cemetery.

"I was just one year older than the oldest of them," she recalled afterward, "and going to look at them made me realize that they had just come of age. You think about how they were just beginning their lives. And then you see those crosses." The seven graves were marked by six white crosses and one headstone, which stated that each of the young miners had died during the first week in October 1918.

In October of 1997, Kirsty Duncan led a team of 15 pathologists, virologists, and excavation experts in a preliminary ground radar survey of the Longyearbyen bodies. Use of the imaging technique enabled the researchers to get an idea of what condition the corpses were in without actually digging them up. Satisfied that the bodies were still frozen, the team scheduled a return visit for the following August.

Once the summer tourist season had ended, the four-nation research team returned to the Longyearbyen cemetery. Wearing biohazard suits and erecting a domelike containment tent, the scientists from Canada, the United States, Great Britain, and Norway performed autopsies on six of the seven bodies. For safety reasons—in case the virus was still live and, upon release from the bodies, possibly dangerous—the autopsies were performed in the coffins while still in the ground. This unusual method was selected in order to reduce the chances that the viral-infected body tissues might defrost, releasing microscopic droplets of the virus into the air.

According to Paul Ewald, a professor of biology at Amherst College and the author of *The Evolution of Infectious Disease*, Duncan's expedition was "one of the most dangerous things people have ever done. My concern is that while it's a valuable study, priority has to be given to safety precautions," he explained in 1997. "The main danger might not be from the bodies themselves but from the clothes. People might have spat up blood and mucus [a common symptom of the 1918 Spanish influenza] on their clothes and the virus might still be present. Frozen fragments of blood could be moderately dehydrated and rise into the air in dust particles."

In order to avoid contact with the victims' bodies and clothing, the researchers used specially shaped biopsy tubes that were inserted into the cadavers. A technique normally used for coring trees, the tube insertion allowed the scientists to remove core samples of frozen tissue from the victims' lungs.

Unfortunately, the six corpses turned out to be badly decomposed, consisting mainly of bones. The permafrost had not kept the ground adequately frozen after all. Still, what samples the researchers could collect were then flown to biohazard laboratories around the world for analysis.

Kirsty Duncan was forced to contend with the massive amount of publicity—much of it negative—

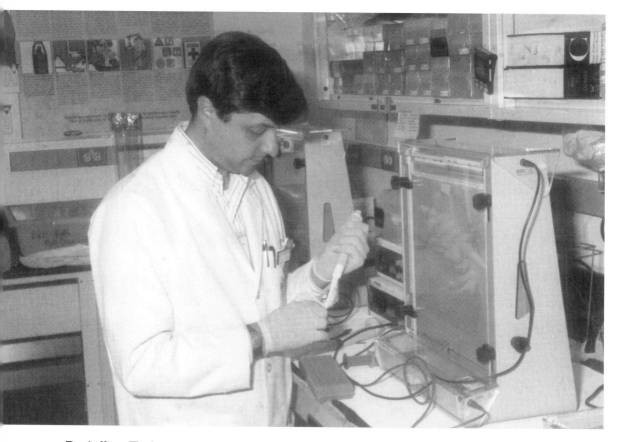

Dr. Jeffrey Taubenberger, chief of the Division of Molecular Pathology at the U.S. Armed Forces Institute of Pathology, discovered the genetic code of the 1918 Spanish influenza virus in 1998.

that her expedition received. Meanwhile, away from the camera lights and reporters' microphones, Dr. Johan Hultin, at age 72, had been digging up bodies in Alaska again.

In March of 1997, Dr. Hultin's desire for adventure had been reawakened by an article in a scientific journal authored by Dr. Jeffrey Taubenberger, the chief of the Division of Molecular Pathology at the U.S. government's Armed Forces Institute of Pathology (AFIP) in Washington, D.C. Along with his colleagues, the 36-year-old Dr. Taubenberger had cracked part of the genetic code for the Spanish influenza virus. Dr. Taubenberger's team had isolated the genetic material known as RNA, or ribonucleic acid, from a sample of diseased lung tissue—tissue that had been saved from 1918 after all.

For close to 80 years, lung tissue samples from 70 soldiers who had died during the 1918 pandemic had sat in the National Tissue Repository, a warehouse run by the AFIP. In 1995, Dr. Taubenberger and his associates decided to search for the influenza virus's genes by autopsying the forgotten samples, and one of the victims' lungs proved useful. A 21-year-old private who had been diagnosed with the flu at a Camp Jackson, South Carolina, base hospital had succumbed soon after. The body tissues of people who died rapidly upon contracting the disease were more likely to harbor the virus, whereas in those who hung on longer, the body's internal defense system typically destroyed the invading microorganisms.

The lung tissue of the army private was stored in a small block of transparent paraffin wax. Over a period of one year, Taubenberger and his team perfected their method for genetic analysis of the tiny piece of tissue. This was an exceedingly tricky task because the genetic material was very fragile. No scientist had ever recovered RNA from a tissue sample so old. Until early in 1996, that is, when Dr. Taubenberger successfully isolated the RNA of the influenza virus from the long-dead private's lungs.

This was certainly a groundbreaking scientific discovery. But in order to develop a complete genetic blueprint, Dr. Taubenberger required more tissue containing the Spanish influenza virus. He had no idea where to find the tissue he needed to continue his research.

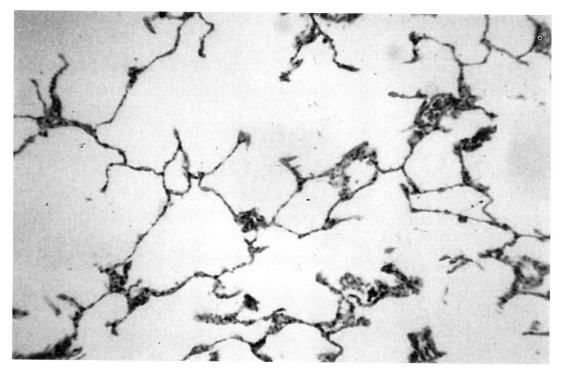

Above: A sample of healthy lung tissue. Facing page: A sample from "Lucy," the Alaskan Spanish flu victim exhumed by Dr. Johan V. Hultin in 1998. Like sponges, the airspaces of victims' lungs filled with fluid, causing the victims to turn blue from lack of oxygen—and sometimes to drown in their own secretions.

Dr. Hultin, of course, knew *exactly* where to dig up that virus-infected tissue. He contacted Dr. Taubenberger and offered to retrieve some frozen lungs from an Alaskan flu victim.

Hultin flew to Alaska, retracing the very same steps he had taken 46 years earlier. Once again, the tribal elders of Brevig Mission granted permission for a dig. (One of the elders Dr. Hultin met during his previous expedition was still living and remembered the scientist.) Using antiseptic procedures and extreme caution, Dr. Hultin unearthed four bodies from the mass grave, including one female corpse that struck him as especially promising. "To the right and left were skeletons," he explained later, "but between them was a beautifully preserved body. It was an obese woman, whose fatty tissue had created an insulation from the surrounding permafrost and protected her organs from occasional short-term thaws."

As an homage to an important fossil skeleton discovered in 1974 in the African nation of Ethiopia, Dr. Hultin named the Alaskan corpse Lucy. He then predicted, "Lucy is going to shed some light on the 1918 influenza pandemic."

Carefully extracting several samples of frozen lung tissue from Lucy, Dr. Hultin packed them in a chemical preservative. When he returned to San Francisco, he shipped the preserved tissue to Dr. Taubenberger in four separate packages to ensure the safe arrival of at least one sample.

Dr. Taubenberger received all four packages with great excitement. Within a few months, his team had successfully decoded the virus's genetic sequencing.

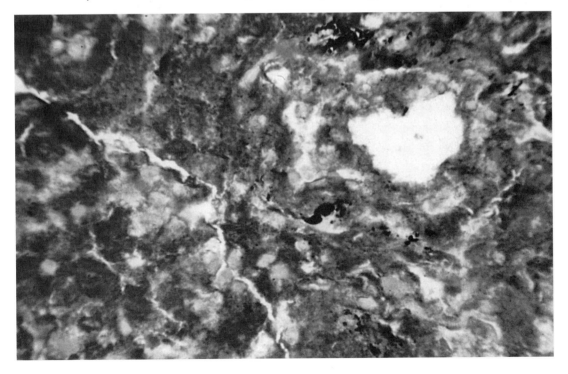

And by June of 1998, they had acquired enough information about the virus's genetic blueprint to allow drug companies to develop a vaccine and anti-influenza drugs that could defeat a modern-day outbreak of the deadly Spanish Lady. Dr. Taubenberger's research team also uncovered all of the genetic information required for creating a vaccine against one of the Spanish influenza's descendants—a new, 21st-century version of the 1918 virus that could appear without warning.

"Working on the 1918 virus is not just some Sherlock Holmes work that we're doing because it's a cool thing to do," says Dr. Taubenberger, a wiry and intense man. "This is a virus that killed tens of millions of people. What if it happened again?. . . This is not just a medical detective story. This could happen again."

In 1997, virologist Robert Webster of St. Jude Children's Research Hospital in Memphis, Tennessee, expressed a similar sentiment in stronger terms. "We need to understand as much as possible about this virus," he said, "because the world will get another pandemic, maybe late in this century or early in the next."

At least now, thanks in large part to Dr. Johan V. Hultin, society can be prepared in case such a frightening global threat ever develops. "It would have been almost impossible to get a sufficient picture of the virus without the Hultin tissue," says Dr. Taubenberger. In the near future, society may be exceedingly grateful to Dr. Taubenberger's team for their lifesaving scientific inroads as well. "This is a tremendous advance," comments Dr. Webster about the genetic decoding. "If this fossil were to reemerge," he says, "we could use this information to get a best-match vaccine that would probably protect us quite well."

"It isn't 'if' it comes back," predicts Dr. Hultin about the killer virus he still obsesses over, "it's when."

After all, some of the deadliest pandemics in the history of humanity have reappeared years later to kill again. And again and again and again.

Early Pandemics:
The First Victims

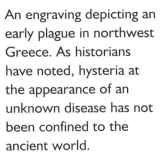

An engraving depicting an early plague in northwest Greece. As historians have noted, hysteria at the appearance of an unknown disease has not been confined to the ancient world.

Fear of a new, unknown disease—especially a deadly disease that strikes large numbers of people—is a deep-seated human emotion. The way society responds to such a profound fear has been relatively consistent throughout history. In the 16th and 17th centuries, for example, the houses of sick people were often boarded up and the afflicted stranded inside, where they were simply left to die. And more recently, equally reprehensible incidents have occurred in which the victims of AIDS have been locked out of their apartments, fired from their jobs, and refused ambulance service.

"We fear what we don't know," says Abraham Lilienfeld, a medical historian and professor of epidemiology (the study of the factors that influence infectious diseases in humans), to explain the historical absence of humanitarian behavior during pandemics. "The social response to the threat of epidemic is extraordinary."

Extraordinarily selfish, that is, and often just plain stupid from fear. This blinding, primitive emotion dooms humans to a paralyzing distrust of one another, creating an atmosphere ripe for the spread of dangerous rumor and misinformation, and for atrociously unneighborly acts. Canadian historian Dr. Anthony Travill calls this destructive attitude "a plague mentality—a fear of the unknown whose size is inversely related to the amount of knowledge we have about the disease." He cites an inherent human trait for the repeated global displays of plague mentality: "Since we cannot blame ourselves we have to blame others."

A look at some of the deadliest epidemics, pandemics, and plagues in recorded history can offer an overview of human behavior in the face of catastrophic medical disaster. Society does not earn high marks in most cases, and it would appear that people's reactions to fear of the unknown remain sadly constant over distance and time.

Between 430 and 429 B.C., a historian in ancient Athens wrote about a devastating disease that afflicted a significant portion of the known world. Modern-day historians credit Thucydides with the earliest record of a plague, although they disagree about what exactly the Plague of Athens might have been.

At first characterized by a mild fever, the mysterious disease turned deadly for victims after a week, causing amnesia, confusion, and paralysis. No one really knows what the epidemic illness was. Some historians today

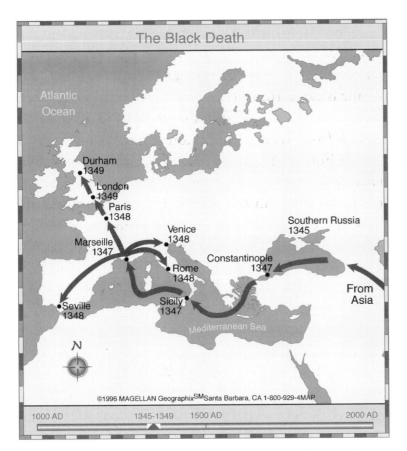

The Black Death

Atlantic Ocean

Durham
1349

London
1349

Paris
1348

Marseille
1347

Venice
1348

Southern Russia
1345

Constantinople
1347

Rome
1348

Seville
1348

Sicily
1347

From Asia

Mediterranean Sea

N

©1996 MAGELLAN Geographix^SM Santa Barbara, CA 1-800-929-4MAP

1000 AD   1345-1349   1500 AD   2000 AD

Map showing the spread of the Black Death. In the 14th century, new overland trade routes and the advent of long-distance shipping helped the bubonic plague—which had originated in Asia—migrate west into Europe. Ultimately the Black Death wiped out up to one-third of Europe's population.

believe it was influenza; others think it might have been the bubonic plague.

Whatever the illness was, it developed during the Peloponnesian War, a bloody and drawn-out conflict between the rival city-states of Athens and Sparta. It is likely that the disease spread rapidly because of the unprecedented contact between large numbers of people who normally did not intermingle.

According to Thucydides, public reaction to the spreading disease was less than noble. "When they were afraid to visit one another," the ancient historian wrote, "the sufferers died in their solitude."

The bubonic plague has returned over and over

throughout history, killing millions. So named because of the appearance of buboes, or large, swollen lymph nodes, on the bodies of victims, the bubonic plague causes high fevers, chills, delirium, and death within days. The first recorded epidemic of this deadly disease may actually have been the Plague of Justinian, which struck in A.D. 542 and lasted until 547. Named after the Byzantine emperor who ruled at the time, the Plague of Justinian swept through Constantinople, producing a death rate that reached an estimated 10,000 people per day. As a survivor recorded at the time, "The whole human race came near to being annihilated. . . . it embraced the entire world."

The bubonic plague was not a viral disease, but a bacterial illness we now know to be caused by the *Yersinia pestis* bacterium. Carried by the fleas of black rats, this microorganism is believed to have originated in the Himalayas. As humans migrated westward through Asia and into Europe, the infected black rats

BACTERIA AND VIRUSES

"Germ" is the word many people typically use to refer to any microscopic disease-causing agent. But germs come in two distinct varieties: bacteria and viruses.

Bacteria are simple, single-cell microorganisms that live in soil, water, the bodies of plants and animals, and almost any organic matter. Their genetic material is DNA, and they can reproduce by themselves. Most do not cause disease.

Viruses are much smaller than bacteria and are unable to live on their own. Composed either of RNA or DNA encased in a protein shell, viruses cannot reproduce by themselves. They reproduce by invading the living cells of another organism and incorporating their own genetic material, influencing the host cell into making more virus.

followed them in search of food.

Bubonic plague struck especially hard from 1346 to 1351, ravaging Asia, wiping out an estimated one-third of the population of Europe, and infiltrating North Africa. The advent of long-distance shipping and extensive overland trade routes may have contributed to the widespread incidence of the plague, referred to at this time as the Black Death because of the black sores that appeared on the skin of victims. Poor sanitation and an inadequate diet also helped to maximize the death rate from this devastating pandemic.

The social impact of the Black Death was quite dramatic. Superstitious and fearful to the point of paranoia, people began to point accusatory fingers at one another, eventually singling out European Jews, who were charged with poisoning the wells. In some horrifying instances of deadly hysteria, Jews were herded into wooden structures and burned alive. The persecution of the Jews, along with other scapegoated minorities, became common practice in the climate of hysteria. At the same time, the death rate and depopulation left a limited supply of skilled workers, such as tradesmen, who were able to demand higher wages. Such social transitions created historic

Hoping to save their daughter, a couple stricken by the bubonic plague give her to friends during the Great Plague of London, 1665. Note the cross above the door at right, which denoted a house containing plague sufferers.

shifts in the patterns of civilization at the time.

Over the next 300 years, bubonic plague recurred sporadically throughout Europe. The last major epidemic of the flea-transported disease struck England in 1665. Referred to as the Great Plague of London, this epidemic occurred when bacteria carried by rats suddenly turned deadly in the filthy slums of London, where people lived crowded together in dirty hovels. Large sections of the city were quarantined, isolated in an attempt to avoid further spread of the disease. Fearing that their pets were carriers of the disease, Londoners exterminated thousands of dogs and cats— which only served to increase the infected rat population because the rats now had fewer predators.

More than 2,000 Londoners died every week for a year until the bubonic plague finally faded away. Some historians attribute the end of the epidemic to the Great Fire of London, which burned down large parts of the city in 1666. Some medical researchers believe that changes in the rat population account for the defeat of the bubonic destroyer. Whatever the reason for its demise, the bubonic plague did nothing to help ease the tensions between wealthy Londoners and their poor neighbors during its reign of terror in 1665.

Bubonic plague is still around, though it rarely strikes. According to the Centers for Disease Control and Prevention (CDC) in Atlanta, which keeps track of the national incidence of infectious diseases, a few cases of bubonic plague are reported in the United States each year.

Between 1485 and 1551, a mysterious disease that became known as sweating sickness terrorized England. The illness exhibited a frighteningly rapid onset, with seemingly healthy victims dying within *two or three hours* of falling ill.

Modern medical researchers have yet to identify the cause of this strange killer disease, but some historians believe it was an influenza virus. Hundreds of thousands of Britons died, including the Lord Mayor of London, his successor, and six aldermen (city leaders). Preferring the homes of the aristocrats to the slums, the killer even dared to invade the royal household: When Anne Boleyn's maid came down with sweating sickness, King Henry VIII did not have her head cut off (as he did with several of his wives and political opponents). Instead, His Royal Highness moved out of his own palace. As one historian reported about the mystery malady, "alarm . . . bordered on maniacal despair."

Toward the end of the 15th century, syphilis first appeared in western Europe. When the disease became epidemic during the 1500s, it existed only in its most virulent form—a far deadlier strain of the sexually transmitted disease than exists today. Back then, syphilis caused flesh and bone to deteriorate rapidly; insanity and death eventually resulted. In the afflicted, large pustules would appear on the skin, and baldness was a common side effect. To advertise their health, young European males began to wear their hair and beards long, which became the fashion as well as a declaration of supposed purity.

Historians blame the sailors returning from Christopher Columbus's expeditions to the New World for the spread of the much-feared new disease. The theory is that the native inhabitants of the West Indies, who had sexual contact with Columbus's men,

Cartoon warning of the hazards of poor sanitation, 1885. In the 19th century, cholera and typhus epidemics killed thousands of Americans.

were the original carriers of syphilis but had developed immunity to the disease. In turn, however, the Europeans infected the aboriginal inhabitants of the New World with diseases to which they had no immunity, including smallpox.

Malaria, too, was pandemic across Europe in the mid-1500s. Typically considered a tropical disease, malaria is a viral illness spread by mosquitoes. The insects suck infected blood from someone who has the disease, then bite someone else—thus passing on the disease. The CDC was established during World War II specifically to deal with the many malaria outbreaks that occurred in combat zones. Although less common today and not a threat in the continental United States, malaria still poses a risk for American travelers.

Travelers in the 1700s returned from the Caribbean with another deadly disease. Yellow fever, a second tropical virus spread by mosquitoes, was so named because of the awful color of victims' skin. Symptoms included fever, nausea, headaches, and internal bleeding, with death soon after. The port cities of Charleston and Philadelphia were hit hard by yellow fever, with 4,000 deaths in the latter city between August and October 1793. Almost a century later, Memphis was devastated by the disease in one of the worst outbreaks in U.S. history. More than 5,000 people—around one-third of the city's population—died of yellow fever in this city on the Mississippi River in 1878.

Between 1817 and 1863, cholera spread from Asia to the rest of the world in four separate waves, becoming pandemic. Typically suffering from severe diarrhea, cholera victims become progressively weaker until they eventually die.

During the Industrial Revolution, with the sudden development of overcrowding in cities and poor sanitation in urban areas, cholera killed thousands of 19th-century Americans. In England, one of the four pandemics left 54,000 dead. In Canada, public fear of the disease turned ugly. According to Geoffrey Bilson, a medical historian at the University of Saskatchewan, "There was . . . a prevailing morality that there were some groups more likely to contract cholera than others, specifically those who lived immorally, the poor and the French Canadian."

Immigrants were automatically quarantined in Canada, which resulted in large numbers of healthy people being exposed to the disease. Makeshift cholera hospitals were set up in various cities, and they often served as targets for public hostility. One angry mob burned down a cholera hospital in Quebec City, and other hospitals were similarly destroyed in London, Ontario, and on Prince Edward Island.

Once it was determined that the disease, which is bacterial in origin, came from unsanitary drinking water supplies, it became possible to prevent further cholera pandemics. In countries where water supplies are kept clean, cholera has almost ceased to exist. In

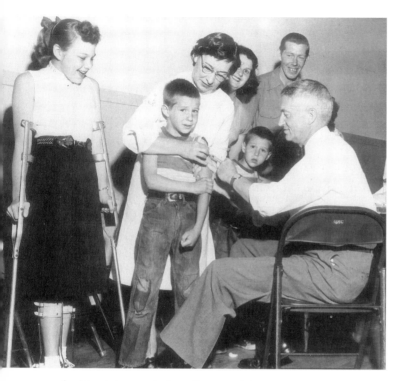

As his sister, a victim of polio, looks on, a six-year-old is vaccinated against the crippling disease, 1955. A successful campaign to vaccinate all children virtually eradicated polio in the United States.

poorer countries where raw sewage often contaminates public water supplies, epidemics of deadly cholera still occur on a regular basis.

Sometime during the 1800s, poliomyelitis, a viral disease causing weakness and paralysis, rose to epidemic proportions in Scandinavia. By 1916, about 9,000 cases had been reported in New York City. Epidemics of polio swept through the entire country during the 1940s and 1950s, when thousands of children (and some older people) lost the use of their arms and legs. Schools were closed, and cities like Milwaukee quarantined all the children in town, restricting youngsters to their own yards in 1944. Between 1915 and 1955, when a vaccine was introduced, approximately 57,000 Americans died from polio. An additional half million survived the disease, many of them needing iron lungs, wheelchairs, or leg braces. Perhaps the most famous polio survivor was Franklin Delano Roosevelt, 32nd president of the United States.

Unlike many of the other epidemic diseases, influenza historically did not—and to a great extent, still does not—elicit much fear. At the turn of the 19th century, the potentially deadly consequences of coming down with the flu were recognized only by a minority, even among medical professionals. A physician's essay printed in the *Journal of the American Medical Association* in 1894, when the United States was in the midst of an epidemic of influenza—also known as the "grippe" or "grip"—tried to correct this situation:

> This disease has been commented upon by some of our ablest men, but it has not received the consideration it deserves, for it extends throughout the habitable world and has destroyed more lives than the cholera and yellow fever put together, attacking alike the centenarian [a person 100 years old or older] and the child within its mother's womb.
>
> Statistics show that railroad employes on freight trains are in more danger than men engaged in battle, yet there is much less dread of enlisting in the railroad service than the military. So also is there less dread of the grip than of cholera or yellow fever, for there are not so many lives lost at one time and in one place. . . .
>
> After tormenting the human race for four years and four months, the grip is as prevalent as ever.

As the hundred-year-old essay makes clear, influenza—though most of us suffer through repeated, mild bouts of it throughout our lives—is a known killer disease. According to *The Handbook of Geographical and Historical Pathology*, influenza "always occurs as an epidemic disease . . . and, indeed, not rarely over a great part of the globe as a true pandemic." The flu is also a mutational disease, which means that the virus itself is always changing. This results in repeated epidemics without a permanent cure for the disease. Unlike polio or yellow fever, for which single effective vaccines have been developed and utilized with great success, the flu virus forces medical researchers to develop new vaccines each time the virus changes.

The influenza virus is extremely contagious. It is often spread by hand-to-mouth contact: someone with the illness covers his or her mouth while coughing, but then shakes the hand of the next flu victim, passing along the live virus in tiny microdroplets of saliva or mucus. Symptoms resemble those of a severe cold, but the flu can develop into bronchitis, pneumonia, and other serious complications involving the lungs. Usually, however, we suffer from the flu for a few days, then rapidly recover full health.

But in 1918, the flu appeared in a most virulent and life-threatening form. For reasons still shrouded in mystery, the common influenza virus suddenly mutated into the most lethal strain ever to stalk the globe. And stalk the globe it did, leaving tens of millions on their deathbeds, blue in the face, blood frothing from slackened mouths.

"As their lungs filled . . . the patients became short of breath and increasingly [blue]," wrote a third-year medical student at the University of Pennsylvania about the patients he was seeing daily in the autumn of 1918. "After gasping for several hours they became delirious and incontinent, and many died struggling to clear their airways of a blood-tinged froth that sometimes gushed from their nose and mouth. It was a dreadful business."

Dr. Albert Lamb, a resident physician in New York, noted how Presbyterian Hospital was operating normally one day but by the next morning had been "inundated with critically ill cases of influenza." It was a ghastly scene. "On admission," Lamb revealed, "most of the early cases were blue as huckleberries. Most of them died. Nearly all were coughing up liquid blood and continued conscious until a short time before death. We had to stand by helpless except for what temporary relief we could give."

Many of the clinical features of the deadly influenza were similar to the symptoms of a typical flu, with the rapid onset of a high fever, headache, muscular pains, sore throat, racking cough, and a general feeling of weakness. However, the 1918 influenza also exhibited ominous new symptoms such as labored breathing, crackling sounds coming from the lungs, the coughing up of blood, bleeding from the nose or mouth, delirium, sleeplessness, and a bizarre blue-black cast to the skin. Flu victims reacted strangely, sometimes flying into crazed rages before collapsing and, usually, dying. And there was a distinctive odor to the 1918 killer flu, a smell like musty straw, "so pungent . . . it just came into your nostrils with a bang," recalled one survivor.

Influenza tends to spread explosively, and in 1918 this meant a worldwide explosion in the onset and ravages of a disgusting, bloody, smelly, and terrifying killer disease. For most people living today, AIDS is the first and only killer disease to have spread across the globe during their lifetime. To learn how society reacted to the threat of the killer pandemic that preceded AIDS, we can turn to historical accounts of the Spanish influenza of 1918. It is indeed a sad, strange, and frightening story.

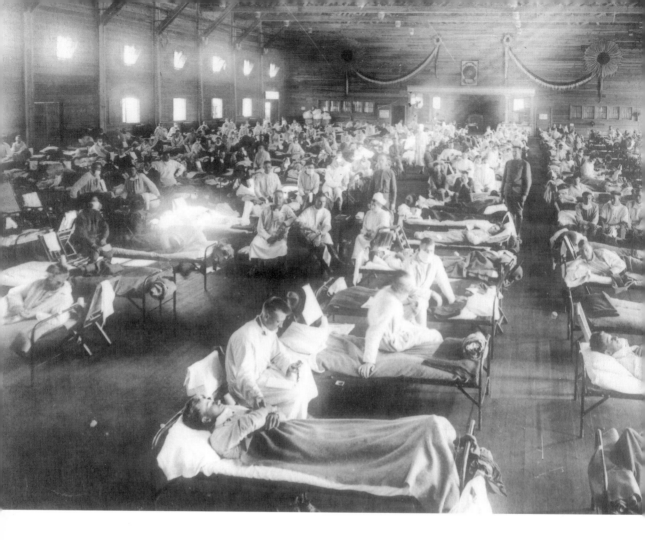

The First Wave:
Influenza Conquers Fort Riley

An emergency hospital at Fort Riley, Kansas—where the first recorded case of Spanish flu occurred in March 1918—overflows with patients.

Historians trace the arrival of the influenza virus in the New World to 1647, when explorer ships traveled to America from Valencia, Spain. Along with a number of other "white man's diseases," influenza disembarked, an uninvited visitor that decided to remain. The well-known British research physician Dr. Willis recorded the symptoms of influenza—which means "influence" in Italian—in 1658: "A feverish intemperature and whatsoever belongs to this . . . thirst, a spontaneous weariness, pain in the head, loyns and limbs, were induced from the blood growing hot and not sufficiently eventilated; hence in many, a part of the thinner blood being heated, and the rest of the liquor being only driven into confusion."

Shortly after the American Revolution, Noah Webster reported that, in his estimation, there had been 44 influenza epidemics since 1174. "The causes," he wrote, "most probably exist in the elements, fire, air and water, for we know of no other medium by which diseases can be communicated to whole communities of people." He determined that influenza was "evidently the effect of some insensible qualities of the atmosphere . . . [an] electrical quality."

Still, no one was very worried about influenza. The two pandemics of influenza that immediately preceded the arrival of the Spanish Lady were relatively mild in America. The first occurred in 1847 and 1848; the second, in 1889, was labeled "Chinese distemper" and attributed by medical authorities of the time to dust from the banks of the Yellow River. These two pandemics did little to ready the world for the devastation that occurred when the Spanish influenza attacked in 1918.

Although it can be difficult to determine later exactly where a pandemic or an epidemic might have started, the first *recorded* case of the Spanish influenza occurred at Fort Riley in Kansas. An old outpost that was used during World War I for training soldiers, the fort sprawled across 20,000 acres of Kansas prairie. On March 9, 1918, a blinding dust storm battered the crowded barracks while gale-force winds blew for three hours.

Fort Riley was intensely busy preparing men to join the American forces battling the German army, so the camp was severely overcrowded with soldiers—and horses. The large number of animals, with their immense piles of manure, had created a serious hygiene problem. A smelly, smoky haze hung over the training camp from the fires kept burning for the daily disposal of the ever-accumulating horse excrement. Not surprisingly, the putrid air caused the soldiers to cough and wheeze. After the dust storm, the mixture of ashes from the burning manure piles and the dust and dirt brought in by the strong wind made for a noxious mess. Soldiers coughed as they cleaned up their filthy quarters in the aftermath of the storm.

Colonel Edward R. Schreiner, a 45-year-old surgeon stationed in Fort Riley, was concerned about the health consequences of the dust storm on the 26,000 soldiers living at the camp. In addition to the lack of heat, hot water, and adequate bathroom facilities, Dr. Schreiner worried about the respiratory effects of breathing in manure ashes mixed with dust. His hospital had a 3,068-bed capacity, and the old limestone buildings were often crowded with soldiers suffering from pneumonia, mumps, measles, and the flu. There had even been a minor outbreak of spinal meningitis, a highly contagious disease that causes vomiting and severe headache, which had afflicted 200 men. But Dr. Schreiner's hospital at the camp had never been filled to capacity.

Before breakfast on March 11, Private Albert Gitchell, a company cook, began complaining about what he believed to be a bad cold. He had a fever, sore throat, headache, and muscle pains. When he reported his symptoms to the hospital duty sergeant, Gitchell was immediately quarantined in a contagious ward. Colds and flus spread rapidly throughout the tightly packed training camp, so every precaution was taken to isolate the men who exhibited the symptoms of a

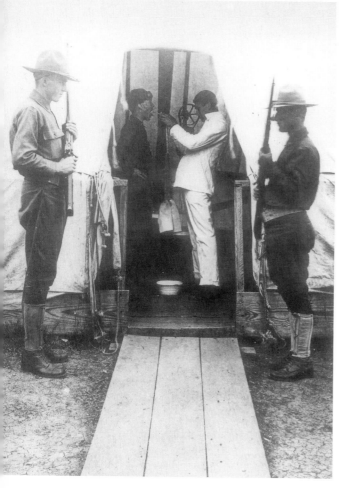

As two sentries stand watch, a military doctor sprays the throat of a recruit. Such preventive measures may have allayed the concerns of soldiers, but they were totally ineffective against the Spanish influenza virus.

communicable illness.

Gitchell had barely stretched out in the hospital bunk assigned to him when Corporal Lee W. Drake reported to the same admitting desk with identical symptoms. And only moments later Sergeant Adolph Hurby stumbled in, coughing fiercely. By the time the chief nurse, Lieutenant Elizabeth Harding, arrived for duty at the hospital, two more sick soldiers were in line for admission. She immediately called Dr. Schreiner.

Before the breakfast dishes were washed in the mess hall at Fort Riley, Dr. Schreiner knew that his post had been hit by an influenza epidemic. By lunchtime, 107 very sick patients had been admitted to the base hospital.

In addition to the typical flu symptoms, Dr. Schreiner noted certain other abnormalities: glandular disturbances, eye aberrations, and a profound depression of all bodily functions and reactions. Even the heart action seemed slowed—a paradox when the body exhibits fever, which usually increases heart rate.

By the end of the week, 522 similar cases had been recorded in the files of the Fort Riley hospital. The army was reporting outbreaks of influenza at other bases, including Camp Kearny, California; Camp Johnson, Florida; Camp Lee, Virginia; Camp McClellan, Alabama; Camp Sevier, South Carolina;

and Fort Oglethorpe, Georgia. The navy reported some 300 cases of flu or pneumonia on ships docked at East Coast ports. Within five weeks, 1,127 soldiers had been stricken at Fort Riley alone; 46 of them had died. The deaths were attributed to pneumonia.

Dr. Schreiner did what he could to improve base hygiene. Screens were installed in the kitchen windows, the plumbing was improved, and oil was poured over the dusty roadways. But the piles of horse manure continued to burn, and the soldiers in training kept on coughing.

The Fort Riley soldiers finished their training, and in May the 89th and 92nd Divisions sailed for France. Soldiers were packed like sardines into the airless hulls of the transport ships, creating an ideal breeding ground for infection. By the time the soldiers landed in France, they had plenty of live flu with them. The American Expeditionary Force, or AEF, called the flu "three-day fever" when it began attacking soldiers stationed in France in the middle of May. The overseas hospitals were soon filled to capacity.

For most of the American soldiers who were in France preparing for an offensive they hoped would end the war, the three-day fever was a mild annoyance. But certain soldiers developed a secondary pneumonia, which sometimes proved deadly. And the three-day fever was extremely contagious. For example, 90 percent of the 168th Infantry Regiment and 90 percent of the sailors at the U.S. Navy Seaplane Station at Dunkirk were affected by this new flu.

In America, where the flu had been limited to soldiers and sailors, the disease had begun to die out by the end of May. But it was just beginning to rage in

Europe, embarking on its first sweep across the entire Old World.

French troops were in the grip of the three-day fever when it was suddenly given a new name—a name that would go down in history. Rolling west over the Pyrenees and into Spain, influenza attacked an estimated 8 million Spaniards during the months of May and June. The nations fighting World War I had censored reports of influenza among their troops to prevent the enemy from gaining valuable information. But because Spain was not involved in the war, it had no censorship. Thus the rest of the world first learned about the massive flu epidemic in Spain, and the disease was dubbed "the Spanish influenza." The Spanish protested that the disease did not originate with them, but crossed the mountains on the winds that blew from the battlefields of France. But the name stuck, and as the deadly influenza that was first seen at Fort Riley made its way around the globe, everyone referred to it as the Spanish influenza or the Spanish Lady.

World War I was a conflict the likes of which the world had never known. After the initial battles in 1914, the fighting in western Europe became a prolonged but horrifyingly bloody stalemate. Both sides dug long systems of trenches along the front lines, and between 1915 and 1917 their respective armies fought over a few miles of territory. Thousands, and often tens of thousands, of men died to move the front a few hundred yards forward, only to see the enemy counterattack and move it back with a similarly obscene loss of life.

In addition to being dangerous, life in the frontline

trenches was difficult and dismal. In his book *War Game*, Michael Foreman described conditions in the trenches:

American soldiers on the front line in France. Cramped conditions in the trenches proved ideal for the spread of influenza.

> The trenches of the Western Front stretched across Belgium and France for a distance of 460 miles. The front trench was about three feet wide at the bottom and seven feet high. To enable the soldiers to fire over or through the parapet, a fire step was built two feet high into the forward side of the trench. It was on this that the sentries stood to keep watch.
>
> Lavatories, or latrines, were dug at the ends of short trenches, mostly to the rear of the main trench. Occasionally they were dug a little way forward into

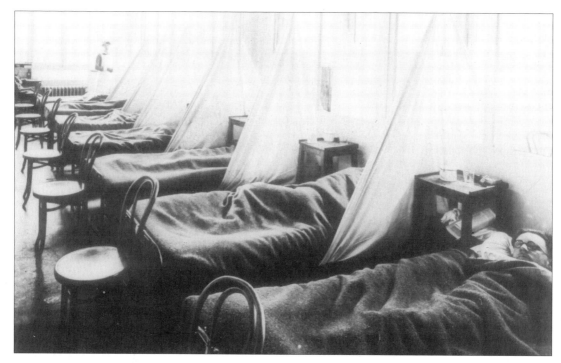

A U.S. military hospital in France. World War I saw the introduction of lethal new weapons and tactics, including poison gas, tanks, massive artillery barrages, and machine-gun crossfire. Yet statistically American soldiers had less to fear from the horrific battlefield than from things they couldn't even see: among the American forces deaths from disease, including the Spanish influenza, exceeded combat deaths by about 20,000.

No-Man's-Land to discourage anyone from lingering too long. . . .

The newcomers quickly learned the routine of trench life. An hour before dawn every morning they received the order to "stand to." Half asleep and frozen, the men climbed onto the fire step, rifles clutched with numb fingers and bayonets fixed. . . .

After an hour or so the order was given to "stand down." Only the sentries remained on the fire step, and the rest of the men enjoyed what breakfast they could get among the rats, blood-red slugs, and horned beetles that infested the trenches.

With the poor sanitation, inadequate diets, and overcrowded and filthy conditions found in the inhospitable environments that awaited the soldiers on both sides of the Great War, it is easy to understand how a contagious disease like the Spanish influenza could spread throughout the troops. The Royal Navy tallied 10,313 cases of influenza as the British were being plagued by bombing raids, food shortages, and casualty lists of increasing length. In a report to the British Ministry of Health, Dr. Herbert French reported on the new disease that had infiltrated the trenches:

> In the midst of perfect health in a circumscribed community, such as a barracks or a school, the first case of influenza would occur, and then within the next few hours or days a large proportion—and occasionally every single individual of that community—would be stricken down with the same type of febrile illness, the rate of spread from one to another being remarkable. The patient would be seized rapidly, or almost suddenly, with a sense of such prostration as to be utterly unable to carry on with what he might be doing; from sheer lassitude he would be obliged to lie down where he was, or crawl with difficulty back to bed so that barrack rooms which the day before had been full of bustle and life, would now be converted wholesale into one great sick room, the number of sick developing so rapidly that hospitals were within a day or two so overfull that fresh admissions were impossible.

The Spanish influenza marched up and down the length of the western front. The French called the malady "purulent bronchitis." The Italians labeled it "sandfly fever." The Germans dubbed it "Blitz Katarrh." In Berlin, 160,000 Germans fell ill. Even Kaiser Wilhelm, the German emperor, was sick with Blitz Katarrh. "It was a grievous business," admitted Germany's leading general, Erich Ludendorff, "having to listen every morning to the Chiefs of Staff's recital of the number of influenza cases, and their complaints about the weakness of their troops." Later, Ludendorff blamed the failure of his important July offensive on the flu that had so weakened his armies.

Soon the intrepid influenza crossed over the German borders into Austria-Hungary, then into Switzerland, where the small Swiss army was almost completely stricken. More than 53,000 cases of Spanish influenza were reported in Switzerland in July 1918. Thousands of cases were reported in Denmark and Norway as well.

Off the southern coast of Spain, funeral processions were winding along the Rock of Gibraltar day and night. The Spanish influenza crossed both oceans, hitting Hawaii, Puerto Rico, and Nome, Alaska. There appeared to be no discernible geographical pattern as the flu jumped aboard destroyers, merchant vessels, and fast trains like the Orient Express, quickly infecting the globe. The Spanish influenza attacked Asia, rolling over much of China "like a tidal wave," according to Dr. Arthur Stanley of the Shanghai Health Department. In Japan, the locals called the disease "wrestler's fever" after it pinned to the mats much of the Imperial Navy.

Sometime during the summer of 1918, as the Spanish Lady flitted around the world leaving crowded hospitals and weakened people of all nationalities in her wake, the nature of the illness itself began to change. Doctors soon discovered that the lungs of those who died from the Spanish influenza harbored a pathological nightmare: hemorrhaging, abscesses, pneumonia, edema (swelling), even complete collapse.

According to Dr. Herbert French of London, "The lung lesions, complex or variable, struck one as being quite different in character to anything one had met with at all commonly in the thousands of autopsies one has performed during the last 20 years."

The Spanish influenza attracted some attention in Europe that summer—certainly more attention than the Americans had paid to it the previous spring. But the disease received only a fraction of the public attention it would have earned—and should have been paid—had the pandemic begun during peacetime. Since the Spanish influenza had started its deadly dance during the Great War, which was of much more interest to most people than "just the flu," it was largely ignored.

Throughout July of 1918, the invisible influenza made increasingly deadly appearances in Russia, North Africa, India, New Zealand, and the Philippines. Rounding the globe in just four months' time—since it had first sent mess cook Albert Gitchell to the base hospital at Fort Riley in Kansas—the Spanish influenza completed its first wave, developing into a killer pandemic, claiming the lives of tens of thousands of victims.

In its second wave, the Spanish influenza of 1918 would kill tens of *millions* of people. Only then would the world begin to recognize the lethal significance of the Spanish Lady.

Tent hospitals for influenza patients, like this one in Lawrence, Massachusetts, sprang up in part because all the regular hospitals were filled to capacity. But some doctors also believed that the "fresh-air treatment" was effective. They were wrong.

The Second Wave:
Influenza Invades America

No place on the face of the globe, it seemed, was safe from the Spanish influenza. The deadly flu infected every continent and virtually every country on the map, going wherever ships sailed or trucks drove or trains traveled. Into the remotest jungles and the most isolated polar regions of the world, the Spanish Lady marched and conquered. Only the tiny island of Tristan da Cunha, located in the South Atlantic Ocean between southern Africa and southern South America, escaped totally untouched by the Spanish influenza of 1918.

The spring wave of the flu had been serious but not disastrous. The second wave was different. After the flu appeared to have died out in midsummer, the illness suddenly resurfaced in late August. It was the

Movie stars Charlie Chaplin (the shorter man at the front of the platform) and Douglas Fairbanks look out over a sea of faces at a Liberty Loan rally. Such huge gatherings fueled the influenza epidemic, but with the war effort in high gear few Americans paid attention to the flu, and public health officials consistently underestimated the dangers.

same flu in that the individuals who had been ill with it in the spring had developed immunity. But the very nature of the flu itself had changed, mutating from a highly contagious but not particularly lethal influenza into a true killer influenza.

The first case of the second wave was recorded at the chief port of disembarkation for the AEF, in Brest, France, on August 22, 1918. Within days, the Spanish influenza appeared in places as far apart as Boston, Massachusetts, and Freetown, Sierra Leone. As it spread around the globe a second time, infecting hundreds of millions of people from Iceland to New Zealand, Samoa to Brazil, doctors and researchers began to share their findings. The grave illness was not "just the flu" this time around, and there was now reason to be alarmed—even scared to death of the new, far more lethal version of the Spanish Lady.

Influenza commonly infects the lining of the respiratory tract, congesting the lungs and sometimes causing pneumonia. But the second wave of the Spanish influenza created much more serious damage in the respiratory tract and lungs. Dr. Jeffrey Taubenberger explained the difference to a journalist from the *New Yorker* in 1997:

> If you autopsied some of the worst cases, you'd find the lungs very red and very firm. The lungs are normally filled with air, so they are compressible. These would be very heavy and very dense. It's the difference between a dry sponge and a wet sponge. A normal piece of lung would float in water because it was basically filled with air. These would sink. . . . These people were drowning. There was so much liquid in the airspaces of their lungs that patients would have bloody fluid coming out of their noses. When they died, it would often drench the bedsheets.

Without adequate oxygen coming into their soaked-sponge lungs, victims' skin would turn blue, a condition called cyanosis. A physician described the discoloration of patients he was seeing in 1918 at Camp Devens in Massachusetts: "Two hours after admission they have the mahogany spots over the cheek bones. And in a few hours you can begin to see the cyanosis extended from the ears and spreading all over the face, until it is hard to distinguish the colored man from the white."

Nurses would have to examine the color of incoming patients' feet in order to determine their race. And those patients whose feet had already turned so blue they were black were usually considered too far gone to be saved.

Another unusual characteristic of this particular strain of influenza was its choice of victims. Flu epidemics typically pose a threat only to the very old and the very young—people who have an immune system that is either weakened from age or not yet well developed due to youth. Young adults may catch the flu, but normally they do not die from it. In 1918, this was not the case. In fact, the Spanish influenza seemed to *prefer* healthy young adults. In the United States, for example, men between the ages of 25 and 29 died from the Spanish influenza at a rate several times greater than that of men between the ages of 70 and 74. The Spanish flu turned virile young soldiers blue overnight, choking them in their own body fluids.

As the summer of 1918 slipped toward autumn, however, most Americans still had no idea of the devastation that would soon overtake the country. Crowds rallied at public meetings and parades intended to raise money for the war effort. Campaigns like "Everybody Sing" and "Liberty Sings" created a party atmosphere in many cities, where most citizens were so consumed with news about the battlefront that they failed to realize the threat facing them on the home front.

In Boston, the summer had been hot and dusty. The Red Sox had won the World Series, and the city was packed with soldiers, sailors, and hordes of civilians visiting the downtown shipyards. Dr. William M. Bryan, a U.S. Public Health Service sanitation officer for the First Naval District in Boston, noted the unsan-

A gauze mask became a required part of the uniform of many public workers, including this New York City street cleaner. While the wearing of masks may have given people a sense of security, the practice probably had little effect on slowing the transmission of the flu, as viruses are small enough to pass easily through gauze.

itary conditions in the naval barracks of South Boston: cracked toilets, lack of drinking fountains, shortages of soap, armies of rats, and a drafty, smelly eating and sleeping area with an overflow of sailors that spilled out from Commonwealth Pier into the lofts of the Army Stores Building. Dr. Bryan found this situation to be "inexcusable." It was also a fertile breeding ground for illness and contagious disease. And, it would turn out, it was the first New World focus of the second wave of the Spanish influenza.

As in many other cities, the civilians of Boston and the soldiers in town awaiting assignment spent plenty of time together. Dr. Bryan wrote of his concerns about this intermixing in a report sent to Washington, D.C. "The congestion of the ship as well as the repeated intercourse with the civilian population," he said, "is believed to be a menace to the health of the personnel and may have its influence upon the present prevalence of influenza."

Actually, it was Bryan's men who were a menace to the civilian population. On the day the doctor submitted his report to headquarters, 58 cases of Spanish influenza had occurred within his command. Ambulances were carrying dozens of feverish soldiers in a steady stream from downtown Boston up the cinder path to Chelsea Naval Hospital, the modern redbrick building overlooking Boston Harbor.

At the end of August 1918, the 1,236-bed hospital was busy with influenza cases. By the end of the first week in September, however, the place had been converted into one vast contagion ward. Tents were pitched on the hospital lawns to hold the overflow of patients, as the number admitted approached twice the bed space of the hospital.

"To avoid the common or garden-variety of the disease," advised an article about Spanish influenza that appeared in the *Boston Globe* newspaper in late summer, "kiss through a handkerchief." It is doubtful that many Bostonians heeded this rather useless advice. The disease was spreading from the enlisted men into the civilian population, with women who worked at the military institutions becoming the first nonmilitary victims.

The first civilian seriously ill with the Spanish flu was admitted to Boston City Hospital on September 3, 1918. On that same day, 4,000 men—including 1,000 sailors from Commonwealth Pier—marched down the streets of Boston in a "Win the War for Freedom" parade. Two days later, thousands of civilians and sailors attended the formal dedication of a new building at the Navy Radio School at Harvard, dancing together until midnight.

On September 11, 1918, the *Boston Globe* ran on its back pages one of the first stories about the spread of infection into the unenlisted ranks: "Catherine Callahan," stated the obituary, "overtaxed by her work for our soldiers, died today." The article then added the telling information that Ms. Callahan's sister and her mother were also in the hospital with pneumonia. Obviously, more than overwork had killed the young volunteer.

Civilian doctors, unlike their military peers, were not required by law to report influenza cases to public authorities. Into the early fall, the medical community chose to downplay the threat of the pandemic for the protection and peace of mind of the general public. Boston's city health commissioner, William C. Woodward, hid his anxiety from his constituents, issuing a bland statement that merely warned people to isolate themselves at the first sign of a cold, to simply get into bed and use over-the-counter cold remedies to treat their symptoms.

But by mid-September, Woodward could no longer remain blasé. He estimated that there were at least 3,000 cases of influenza in the city of Boston, and on September 18, a total of 40 deaths had occurred within

To avoid bringing people together in a closed room, this court in San Francisco was moved outdoors during the height of the pandemic.

a 24-hour period. Woodward was finally forced to admit that with "the grippe making headway in every neighborhood, rich or poor, there was nothing to be gained by denying its presence."

At Corey Hill in the Brookline section of Boston, health department employees and soldiers had worked together to pitch a tent hospital, where a vast expanse of canvas tents served to house the incoming masses of flu patients. Fire hydrants were used as water taps, and white-uniformed nurses bent over the squat water sources, filling pitchers. Other towns followed suit, erecting the makeshift hospitals on empty lots that soon resembled circus encampments.

In Boston, the Liberty Loan parades were post-poned. The city streets grew quiet as the raspy sound of coughing and the delirious voices of fevered victims filled the rooms of tenements and townhouses. By this time, doctors had noted that there were three types of influenza victims:

1. In the first type, the disease began mildly and the patients felt as though they would be better in a couple of days. A day or two later, there was a rise in tempera-ture followed by the onset of pneumonia, then death.

2. In the second type, the disease began in a some-what severe form, followed by complications in the lungs, then recovery.

3. The third type began with extremely severe symptoms. Breathing became very difficult, cyanosis set in, and the lungs filled with liquid; patients were drowning in their own fluid, their faces blue from lack of oxygen. In this type, death followed in 36 to 48 hours.

By October, panic had set in within the city of Boston. By the 16th, more than 3,700 people had died from influenza. Doctors and nurses were in short sup-ply. The city's newspapers ran front-page requests for volunteers—healthy men and women willing to work as nurses, bandage stitchers, ambulance drivers, laun-derers, pharmacists, and messengers. Henry Endicott, the acting chairman of the Emergency Public Health Committee, asked that people "step forward and show their patriotism." But it was a new war he was recruit-ing for now. This battle was being waged against the invisible enemy—the Spanish influenza.

The city was forced to close the public schools because so many teachers were out sick. Other public services were failing, too. The Boston Street Railway had so many men absent that the trains were rarely on schedule. More than 850 telephone operators were too ill to work, so Bostonians were advised to limit their phone use to emergency calls only. In Quincy, just south of Boston, shipbuilding halted as scores of ship workers fell ill. In one afternoon, three men dropped dead on the sidewalks of Quincy.

In downtown Boston, authorities closed the city's theaters in an attempt to limit contact between people. Even the soda shops and saloons were shut down. Although hotels and cabarets remained open, dancing was prohibited.

The city morgue experienced a backup of unprecedented proportions. There weren't nearly enough coffins to meet the city's needs, and grave diggers couldn't keep up with the rapidly mounting stacks of dead bodies. Wakes were discouraged, and though funerals were generally kept small, an incessant parade of coffins and black-clad mourners wended through the otherwise deserted city streets.

In October of 1918, Francis Russell was a third grader at the Martha Baker School in the Dorchester section of Boston. Free to play all day long because the influenza pandemic had closed his school, Francis listened as the horse-drawn funeral carriages rolled by, and he watched as the coffins piled up in the chapel at the local cemetery, where a tent had been set up to house the overflow. One autumn eve, upon sneaking into the cemetery to watch a funeral and being chased away by a white-haired stranger, the boy walked home, deep in contemplation. Years later, Russell wrote about the personal significance of that moment:

"In that bare instant I became aware of time. And I knew then that life was not a perpetual present, and that even tomorrow would be part of the past, and that for all my days and years to come I too must one day die."

Boston continued to serve as one of the focal points of the Spanish influenza infection, with outbreaks elsewhere in the United States being traced back to infected soldiers coming from the Massachusetts capital. At first, U.S. public officials held out hope that the second wave would limit itself to New England, or even to the section of the country east of the Mississippi. But the flu traveled fast—to wherever infected people went. As Dr. Hermann M. Briggs, then New York State's public health commissioner, explained: "The rapidity of the spread of influenza throughout a country is only limited by the rapidity of the means of transportation. The disease is carried from place to place by persons, not things. Its rapid extension is due to its great infectivity, the short period of incubation, usually two days or less, the mild or missed cases, and the absence of precautionary measures."

The second wave of the Spanish flu eventually washed over most of the military bases in the United States. In Camp Devens, more than 5,000 soldiers were afflicted with the second round of influenza. At Fort

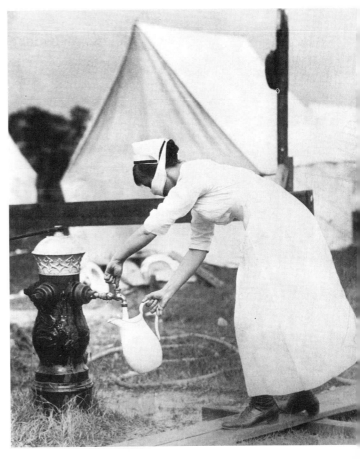

A nurse draws water from a hydrant at the Corey Hill tent hospital for servicemen in Brookline, Massachusetts.

Riley, the flu had returned for a deadly round two. New Orleans quarantined Fort St. Philip, allowing no one to enter or leave the small post. In San Francisco, the United States Naval Training Station on Goat Island was under quarantine. Drinking fountains were sterilized hourly with blowtorches, telephones were cleansed with alcohol, and trainees were forced to march 20 feet apart. The soldiers' throats were smeared with silver nitrate, their noses sprayed with another preventive solution. No enlisted men were allowed to venture into the city.

But it was too late for even the most severe restrictions to stem the tide. The Spanish flu had already infected soldiers and civilians alike, and the second wave continued its deadly sweep across America throughout the fall of 1918. In one town in New Hampshire, 36 young mothers died from the flu. Pregnant women in New York, Washington, Philadelphia, and elsewhere suffocated as they struggled to breathe for two. Strong men, strapping young specimens of vigor and health, died overnight in cities and towns all over the country. "The husky male either made a speedy and rather abrupt recovery or was likely to die," reported Dr. Victor C. Vaughan, the surgeon general of the army in 1918. "Nature overdoses the resistance, kills the invading organisms too rapidly, and sets free such an amount of poison that death occurs. . . . Infection, like war, kills the young, vigorous, robust adults."

Half the population of Watkins, New York, fell ill. The high school principal took over as chief cook in the town's largest auditorium, which had been converted into a hospital.

In the Upper Peninsula of Michigan, Annie L.

Colon, a public health nurse, used a handcar to travel to the homes of the stricken. Accompanied by a doctor and carrying soup, bread, blankets, bedsheets, and bottles of aspirin, quinine, cough syrup, whiskey, gin, and rum, she visited the sick who were isolated in remote lumber camps. "We have had a terrible time in this county, losing 100 people or one person out of every 50," Nurse Colon reported to the State Health Department in Lansing. "We rode 20 and 30 miles at night through the deepest woods and over the roughest roads to camps, and many times we would find 30 or 40 cases, sometimes 10 people all huddled together fully drest [sic] in a tiny log cabin, probably all in two beds and all with fevers over 104°."

In Columbus, Ohio, policemen were assigned to ride the trolleys and limit the number of riders, in the hope of restricting contact. In Wilmington, Delaware, 3,000 residents were in bed with the flu. Delaware College sealed up its campus. In Chicago, soldiers of the Home Guard patrolled closed school yards, saloons, and movie theaters. Dr. C. St. Clair Drake, the director of the Ohio State Department of Public Health, ordered all hospital attendants to wear masks over their noses and mouths to prevent the spread of germs. In Seattle, policemen were required by law to wear masks at all times. But nothing—no law, no ordinance, no closing, no facial covering—could halt the spread of the Spanish influenza.

In the fall of 1918, the Spanish Lady was killing more Americans than the Great War in Europe. And there was no end in sight. Elsewhere, the deadly flu continued its offensive on a worldwide battlefront. No nation was spared.

Masks and Onions: Theories and Remedies but No Cure

5

Medical researchers and historians can look back on the world health crisis that occurred in the autumn of 1918 and nod their heads. Any major social upheaval, we now realize, can serve as a breeding ground for worldwide infection. The Spanish influenza of 1918 most likely owes its unprecedented lethal success to the concurrent incidence of the First World War.

Paul Ewald, the Amherst College biologist, explains such a connection in his book *The Evolution of Infectious Disease*. Normally, Ewald notes, people are much more likely to catch a mild flu than a very severe flu because they are much more likely to run into someone else who has the mild form—those ill with a serious influenza infection stay home in bed or are hospitalized. But in 1918, this rule of thumb didn't apply because there was a war going on. Wars— like urban overcrowding and refugee camps—provide influenza strains with the opportunity to infect large numbers, and to mutate and strengthen.

The mild form of Spanish influenza was passed from soldier to soldier during the spring wave of 1918. When the soldiers moved about in crowded transport ships and trains, with the ill amassing in overcrowded hospitals, the infection began to spread wildly. The 1918 flu traveled everywhere the soldiers were sent, which, during wartime, was just about everywhere in the world. And the mild influenza strain soon strengthened, developing into a killer strain before finally dying out on its own. If everyone had been home in bed recovering from the nasty flu, instead of flocking to the "Liberty Sings" galas and kissing soldiers on dirty, dusty street corners, perhaps the spring wave would have played itself out while largely confined to barracks and trenches.

But that is not what happened in 1918.

November proved to be a particularly gruesome month. In Rio de Janeiro, Brazil, one man asked another where the streetcar stopped, thanked him, then fell over dead—from the Spanish flu. In Cape Town, South Africa, seven riders on a train collapsed and died from the flu within a three-mile stretch. And in Johannesburg, South Africa, a machine operator was moving a steel cage full of gold miners up from a deep underground mine when he was suddenly paralyzed, stricken by the Spanish influenza. The cage kept coming up, smashed into the overhead frame, and fell back into the mine shaft. Twenty-four miners

plunged to their deaths in the tragic accident.

In Cape Town, people who dared to walk the deserted streets were horrified as their neighbors collapsed and died right in front of them. A young boy who was riding into the city on a train reported spotting "bodies . . . scattered about on the expanse of field," stretching as far as he could see. Wooden carts were piled high with corpses, the legs of the dead sticking out from under the tarpaulin covers, labels attached to the feet to identify bodies on their way to the cemetery. Each morning, the city wagons drove about, collecting bodies from the streets and from homes where deaths had been reported, the cart drivers calling, "Bring out

Dancers at a potlatch (ceremonial feast), Chilkat, Alaska. On November 7, 1918, Governor Thomas Riggs Jr. issued a directive outlawing potlatches and urging Alaskan natives to discard their traditions of hospitality. Nevertheless, Alaska was decimated by the Spanish influenza.

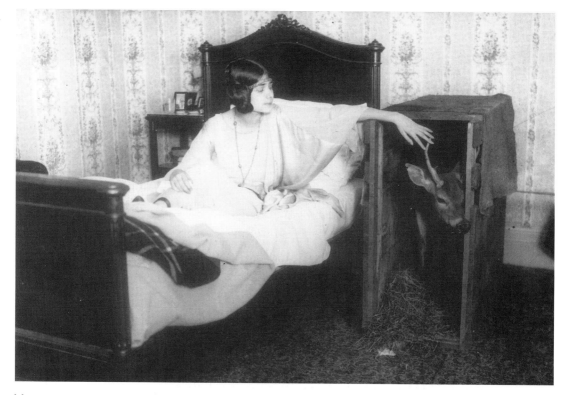

Home remedy: keep a live deer by the bed. As the death toll mounted and hysteria gripped communities everywhere, a host of absurd flu treatments sprang up.

your dead!" As one observer, a 21-year-old student at the University of Cape Town in 1918, recalled decades later, "Cape Town was a veritable city of the dead."

In the black neighborhoods of Kimberley, an old South African mining town, poor sanitation and over-crowding added to the death toll, which far exceeded the citizens' ability to handle all the corpses. The roads to the town cemetery were soon filled with carts piled high with bodies wrapped in blankets or sacks. As one survivor described it, the streets were full of "heart-breaking sights—a brother pushing his bicycle with his dead sister wrapped in a sheet . . . a husband pushing a wheelbarrow with his wife's body in a home-made box." Fear, grief, and depression pervaded the town. A postal official told the local newspaper in November

1918 that it was "impossible for me to describe the consternation and depression of spirits that existed amongst those who were not struck down with the malady. We were all wondering whose turn it would be next to be carted away."

In Tahiti, 3,000 citizens fell ill in November of 1918. One-quarter of the island population died within 25 days. The Samoa Islands, located 4,000 miles from San Francisco, were also hit hard by the second wave of the pandemic. In Western Samoa, approximately 20 percent of the total population—7,542 islanders—died in less than two months. The epidemic had completely paralyzed the islanders' ability to procure and distribute food, so many of the flu deaths were hastened by starvation. New Zealanders referred to the month of sickness and death on their islands as "Black November."

In Juneau, Alaska, the city government advised all citizens to "keep as much to yourself as possible" when the flu epidemic struck in the fall of 1918. The disease spread anyway, thanks in large part to the customs and traditions of the Alaskan culture. Governor Thomas Riggs Jr. issued a directive on November 7 advising all Alaskan natives not only to discard their traditions of communality and hospitality and to stay in their own villages, but also to refrain from visiting one another's homes and to avoid all gatherings. "A potlatch is absolutely forbidden, and any Native attempting to get up a potlatch will be prosecuted," warned the advisory.

In the Nome area, few Eskimos escaped the flu. Some fled from cabin to cabin, infecting one another at each stop. Rescuers found entire families who had frozen to death, too ill to rebuild their fires. When a group of Eskimos were housed in a single building to be cared for by medical volunteers, several natives saw their rescue as incarceration in a death house and hanged themselves. In a report to the secretary of the interior, Governor Riggs wrote that, in his opinion, the Spanish Lady had been at her cruelest and most devastating in Alaska. "I doubt," Riggs said, "if similar conditions existed anywhere in the world—the intense cold of the arctic days, the long distances to be traveled by dog team, the living children huddled against their dead parents already being gnawed by wolfish dogs."

While the pandemic continued to wreak havoc around the world, the cause of the disease remained a mystery, eluding the best medical research of the era. Likewise, proven medical treatments didn't exist. That is not to say, however, that opinions on the subject were hard to find. Everybody, it seemed, knew what brought on the disease and what could prevent or cure it.

Lieutenant Colonel Philip S. Doane, head of the Health and Sanitation Section of the Emergency Fleet Corporation, discussed with the press a widespread rumor that the pandemic might have been started by German spies. "It would be quite easy," Doane observed, "for one of these German agents to turn loose Spanish influenza germs in a theater or some other place where large numbers of persons are assembled. The Germans have started epidemics in Europe, and there is no reason why they should be particularly gentle with America." Most American newspapers printed the story.

Schoolchildren had a simpler theory. In playgrounds throughout the country, children had begun jumping rope to a new song:

I had a little bird
And its name was Enza.
I opened the window
And in-flew-Enza.

Mother knows best? These boys' parents have outfitted them with bags of camphor, an insect repellent, to ward off the flu.

But many Americans chose to blame the Germans for the devastating illness that had virtually shut down the major cities of America. "Let the curse be called the German plague," one patriot told the *New York Times*. "Let every child learn to associate what is accursed with the word German not in the spirit of hate but in the spirit of contempt born of the hateful truth which Germany has proved herself to be." The U.S. Public

Health Service tested Bayer aspirin tablets to disprove the popular rumor that the product, developed under a German patent, was poisoning users with flu germs.

Some blamed the pandemic not on the Germans but on the war itself. "There is so much [poison] gas in use over there that the air around the world is poisoned," wrote H. E. Hamilton to the U.S. surgeon general in November 1918. Others pointed to the poor diet, poverty, and decline in sanitation brought on by the war. Dr. Albert J. Croft of Chicago held a more complex belief:

> The numerous gases used on the battlefields of Europe, with their highly poisonous properties, the liberation of a large quantity of ground air high in carbon dioxide content due to trench systems, the gases from decomposing bodies and lower animals, and those set free by the destruction of cities and ammunition dumps during the last few years, may have combined to form a gaseous compound with highly toxic properties probably due to the rearrangement of molecules by the tremendous concussion produced by high explosives.
>
> With this idea in mind I am going to advance the theory that the condition termed influenza is in reality a non-bacterial, non-contagious disease caused by the inhalation of small amounts of a depressing, highly irritating, high density gas, present in the atmosphere, especially at night and when the air is supercharged with moisture, more particularly near the surface of the earth.

In South Africa, white fingers pointed to black faces as racism caught the Spanish flu. Exposés, letters, editorials, and articles by white citizens were published in newspapers, accusing the black slums and their unsanitary conditions of causing the epidemic of influenza.

Many South Africans believed that the illness was spread by the wind. Scary stories circulated that a dark rain accompanied the disease, and that baboons and birds were also dying from the flu. Individuals of various religious affiliations attributed the pandemic to God's direct action, either as a punishment or for some divine purpose. Some felt that the sins being punished by influenza were highly specific, including a straying from God, indifference, unbelief and superstition, failure to attend church, and the worshiping of science. Others felt that the pandemic was a divine means for ending a devastating war.

Like Americans, the South Africans also placed blame directly on the Germans. According to the *Cape Times*, information had been provided by "a high medical authority . . . that Spanish influenza may be directly traced to the use of poison gas by the Germans . . . apparently another penalty which civilization has to pay for the prostitution of German science to the service of the Devil." Even though only a small proportion of the South African population was actively involved in World War I, the bloody warfare in Europe had made a deep impression on the country—and the rest of the world watching the black-and-white films and newsreels that showed the largest and most ferocious war in history being waged with the most horrific weapons ever invented.

Medical researchers believed that the Spanish influenza was caused by a specific bacterium, Pfeiffer's bacillus, because they had isolated this germ from the lungs of victims. Actually, Pfeiffer's bacillus produced secondary infections only, invading the respiratory tracts of victims already weakened by the Spanish influenza. More than a decade would pass before scientists discovered that the Spanish influenza was actually a viral disease.

In 1918, however, armed with their widely accepted and completely wrong theory, medical researchers developed vaccines. In the late fall, physicians in Philadelphia, Boston, Chicago, New York, and many other cities and towns began to inoculate people who had not yet come down with the flu. Since the vaccines didn't boost immunity to the virus that actually caused the Spanish influenza, they did little besides calm recipients' nerves. Still, the vaccines seemed to be effective. In fact, everything being used to fight the Spanish flu appeared to be increasing in effectiveness. But this was only because the second wave of the pandemic had started to run its natural course.

Despite the ineffectiveness of the remedies, nearly everyone touted a surefire method for curing the sick of the Spanish influenza. The surgeon general of Massachusetts, Dr. William A. Brooks, believed in the curative value of sunshine and fresh air, so he moved stricken servicemen to the tent hospital on Corey Hill. Other medical authorities ridiculed this treatment method as "barbarous." Later, studies showed that ill soldiers in tent wards fared no better than victims who remained in overcrowded barracks. But fewer people *caught* the Spanish flu in the outdoor structures.

Most medical professionals advised flu patients to stay in bed, keep warm, and drink plenty of fluids. The surgeon general of the U.S. Public Health Service issued a statement to the press recommending bed rest, good food, salts of quinine, and aspirin for those with the flu. Millions of fliers repeating this sensible advisory were circulated by Public Health Service employees. However, the campaign did not dispel the rampant rumors of special flu curatives, which spread across the country as rapidly as the disease.

In the Midwest, sick lumberjacks curled up with bottles of whiskey. In Los Angeles, victims made flannel bags containing the bitter plant wormwood, which they soaked in hot vinegar before applying to the chest. "Rinse the mouth with lime water, inhale hot water and turpentine fumes," suggested one daring citizen of Leavenworth, Kansas. Dr. Charles E. Page of Boston shared his unique theory with the *New York Herald*: "Influenza is caused chiefly by excessive clothing on an animal by nature naked." His proposed cure: go naked. "The skin," Page opined, "is a true breathing organ; its millions of blood vessels are forever gasping for air under even the lightest of drapery."

The best antiflu formula, advised a woman from Pasadena, California, was a knockout combination of alcohol and chloroform. In Amarillo, Texas, another inhalation formula, supposedly recommended by a wise old Mexican man, included smoke from slow-burning wood, damp straw, or hay. Dr. Alexander B. Leeds of Chickasha, Oklahoma, announced that the Spanish flu could be cured by removing the patients' tonsils—and teeth.

"Stop circulating books!" was the wild advice spread around New York City. The public library closed its doors.

"Stop shaving!" was another hysterical advisory. In

During the pandemic, it was the lawmen who wore masks and the outlaws who didn't. In some places not wearing a mask in public was an offense punishable by a fine or jail sentence.

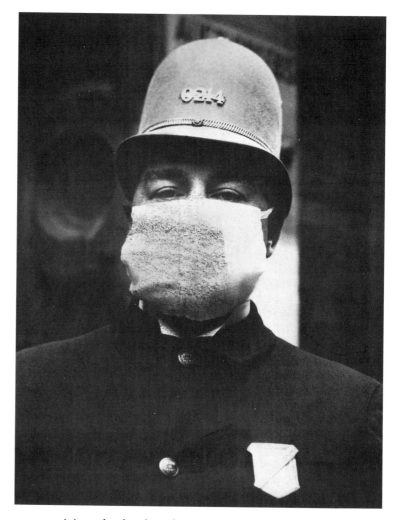

many cities, the barbershops were shut down, and men turned to safety razors or simply grew beards.

"Wear fresh pajamas!" the self-proclaimed experts advised. Take castor oil! Don't take castor oil! Rest! Exercise! Eat ice cream! Avoid sugar! Drink fluids only! The advice poured into households as fast as the flu patients sank into hospital beds.

Mrs. Ann Olds Woodson of South Chicago wrote directly to the War Department:

Take two or three large, ripe but fresh red peppers of the hot variety (not the sweet variety), chop fine, put them in an open stew pan with plenty of water to cook them—set on the stove and boil nicely for an hour or more, or two hours would be better, keeping enough water to prevent their burning or getting dry.

Have outside windows and doors closed, or mostly so, the object being to permit the vapor to permeate all the air of the living apartments that the patient may inhale this impregnated air as strongly as he can take of it for the time stated above. This will cause a loose- ness of the cold and a coughing and sneezing. . . . Either it kills the germs of disease or causes the system to throw it off.

In some cases, a second treatment might be needed.

In a syndicated news column on the topic of health, a reader who signed himself "S.Q." shared his own dietary cure: "The morning I noticed the symptoms, I drank two quarts of hot water and I started spraying my nose and throat—my diet has been milk and bran and fruit, except the hot water I drank occasionally. Each morning when my head was stuffed and throat sorest I drank two quarts of hot water and I immedi- ately felt like a new man. On the fourth day, I was practically well."

One enterprising cook, a Pennsylvania homemaker, served massive amounts of onions to her family. All eight avoided contracting the Spanish flu. A frightened mother in Portland, Oregon, buried her four-year-old daughter in raw sliced onions. Desperate people adopted all sorts of silly home remedies, from tying slices of cucumber to their ankles to carrying a potato in each pocket. The hopeful fashioned small cloth bags to be worn around the neck, which they filled with camphor, an insect repellent. In New Orleans, residents resorted to voodoo charms and chants, such as "Sour, sour, vinegar V, keep the sickness off of me."

Facial coverings that resembled the surgical masks worn by doctors were used, mandated by city ordinances in certain parts of the country. In Tucson, Arizona, a judge fined a window washer for removing his mask to blow-dry the glass panes. In San Francisco, all "mask slackers" were fined $100 or sent to jail for 10 days. The police wore small gauze pads over their noses and mouths, which the *San Francisco Chronicle* described as "resembling in size and contour about nine ordinary slabs of ravioli arranged in a square of three each way."

Many doctors and medical researchers believed that the use of masks was absurd. As Dr. John F. Kyle of California explained, "Masks are for doctors and nurses in an operating room. They look good to the poor innocent patient. . . . Influenza is a self-limited disease and it gets you going or coming regardless of vaccines or mask."

A committee of pathologists appointed by the Massachusetts State Board of Health reported that, according to their research, "the vaccines we have considered have no specific value in the treatment of influenza." Equally useless was "Grippura," a Spanish flu tonic sold to the naive, and "Spanish Influenza Remedy," offered on the streets of South Chicago by snake oil salesmen who actually employed a turbaned snake charmer to draw crowds of potential buyers. The truth, however, did not slow down the advocation of a wide array of treatments. Plenty of money was made by pharmacists and quacks alike, some with good intentions, others with pure profit in mind.

In Brazil, flu-threatened citizens drank large quantities of rum, and the sultry cafés of Rio de Janeiro remained open, even as the unluckiest of the residents were dropping dead all around. In Paris, Dr. Louis St. Maurice, a society doctor, advised everyone to wear a nightcap. Dr. Roland Burkitt was known as "Kill or Cure" in Nairobi, Kenya, where he placed flu patients between cold wet sheets and doused them with frigid water. In Tibet, healers drummed day and night to prevent sick people from sleeping, which they believed would result in death. All over the world, people prayed.

In reality, there was very little any medical professional—or anyone else, for that matter—could do about the Spanish influenza. In fact, in 1918 no one knew what to do to help slow down the spread of the killer disease, to prevent it from infecting people, or to cure them when it did. Fortunately, the pandemic eventually eased up its assault on its own, and by late November, the Spanish Lady appeared to be taking a break from dancing on graves all over the globe.

Scenes like this one in New York City were played out on street corners across the country as Americans celebrated the end of World War I, November 11, 1918. Though by then it also seemed that the Spanish flu was defeated on the home front, a third wave of the pandemic would soon sweep the country.

Armistice and the Third Wave

"Everything is overflowing with patients," wrote Dr. George Washington Crile, a surgeon with the U.S. Army's Mobile Hospital No. 5, stationed in Europe during World War I. "Our divisions are being shot up; the wards are full of machine-gun wounds. There is rain, mud, 'flu' and pneumonia."

"I have been operating on twelve-hour shifts here," Crile continued. "One hundred and twenty cases are waiting for operation this morning. In one night I had 60 deaths."

The spark that had ignited World War I occurred on June 28, 1914, when Archduke Francis Ferdinand of Austria-Hungary was assassinated by Serbian terrorists. Backed by Germany, Austria-Hungary declared war on Serbia on July 28. Within a week, alliance obligations and political considerations had pulled Europe's major powers—Germany, Russia, France, and Great Britain—into the conflict. All of Europe was at war.

At the outbreak of the war, the United States was a neutral nation. Gradually, however, public opinion turned against Germany, though the United States stayed out of the European war. When Germany launched a campaign of unrestricted submarine warfare—sinking all vessels, including those of neutral countries—President Woodrow Wilson could no longer keep America out of the conflict. On April 2, 1917, President Wilson stated that the intention of the United States in entering World War I would be to make the "world safe for democracy." On April 6, 1917, Congress declared war.

Major General John J. Pershing, the commander in chief of the AEF, believed that the American army needed one million men in France by May of 1918. American troops were sent overseas as soon as transport ships were available, so some soldiers arrived in Europe fully trained, while others had yet to be taught how to load a rifle. By the summer of 1918, the American troops were being tested in battle, joining the French in a major offensive on September 12, then battling through the autumn to their eventual, final victory. At daybreak on November 11, 1918, the Germans signed a general armistice. Six hours later, on the 11th hour of the 11th day of the 11th month, the guns stopped firing. The ghastly war was finally over.

World War I had unleashed unprecedented suffering and destruction. More than 15 million soldiers,

Two young women disinfect the sidewalk after passersby flouted the instructions on the sign.

sailors, and airmen lost their lives; millions more were wounded and maimed. Throughout the European front, massive artillery shelling had leveled cities, towns, and villages, and civilian deaths from the conflict have been estimated at more than 12 million. Although it entered the fighting late in the war, the United States lost more than 53,000 men in battle. Illness, including the Spanish influenza, claimed the lives of an additional 73,000 American soldiers.

Not surprisingly, the end of the carnage was greeted with jubilation throughout the world. Many people believed that this "war to end all wars" would indeed mark the last time that men ever took up arms against one another. And, by happy coincidence, with the signing of the armistice the second wave of the epidemic of Spanish flu began to recede throughout Europe. The disease had already been dying out in America, where cities and towns were gradually coming back to life. Theaters and saloons, shops and schools were open for business again as the sick recovered and fewer and fewer people fell ill.

At dawn on Armistice Day, American factory whistles blew, fire bells clanged, church bells rang, and guns were fired into the air. By midmorning, every city in America was celebrating the end of the war. In Chicago, people of all ages paraded through the city decked out in costumes. In New York City, any soldier who ventured into Times Square was kissed passionately by throngs of jubilant, grateful women. The carillons in the churches of Pittsburgh played "Johnny Get Your Gun" and "Over There," two songs popularized during the war. Young children tied tin cans to the tails of thousands of dogs and cats, which ran through the city, clattering over the cobblestones.

In most towns, the celebration continued throughout the day and into the night. In their belief that they had been liberated from both the terrors of war and the ravages of the Spanish influenza, overjoyed Americans partied and paraded, sang loudly and drank toast after toast, and danced and kissed one another exuberantly.

In fact, only the war was really over. A third wave of the Spanish influenza, more virulent than the first wave but milder than the second, would develop by the end of the year. But all of America, believing that the crisis had passed, chose to defy the public health rules in favor of hugging, kissing, dancing, and partying.

People needed to reconnect with their neighbors, to begin to trust one another again instead of regarding everyone as a potential infector. As fear had spread during the peak of the pandemic, violence and vigilantism had flourished. In certain towns in New Mexico, for example, strangers disembarking from trains were told to move on. In her autobiography, author Mary McCarthy described how her dying father had pointed a pistol at a surprised conductor who was trying to eject the ailing McCarthy family from a train headed to Minneapolis. In Montana, a rancher hijacked a busy doctor, forcing him at gunpoint to treat his flu-stricken family. Masks were used more successfully by robbers than by law-abiding citizens.

The laws grew extraordinarily strict in those cities where the Spanish flu had gradually begun to terrorize public officials. In Chicago, landlords whose tenants died after the heat was turned off for nonpayment of rent were charged with murder—if the tenants had been ill with influenza. New York City doctors were fined when they failed to report flu cases to the public health authorities. Hundreds were arrested for spitting in public, and America's new public enemy number one was the "open-faced sneezer," who ignored laws and refused to wear a mask. In Prescott, Arizona, shaking hands was ruled a jailable offense. The public health officer in San Francisco received a handmade bomb in the mail, a telling response to his unpopular laws requiring all citizens to wear facial masks in public.

In Chicago, laborer Peter Marrazo became insane from the devastation the Spanish influenza had caused his family. As rescuers battered their way into his apartment through a barricaded door, they could hear

President Woodrow Wilson reviews American troops in France on Christmas Day 1918. Wilson would be stricken by the Spanish flu during the Paris Peace Conference. Though he survived, some historians think his brush with influenza left him permanently weakened—physically as well as mentally.

him screaming, "I'll cure them my own way!" Marrazo slashed the throats of his sick wife and four ill children. Some fear-crazed individuals called in medical professionals to treat their stricken family members, then fled their own homes in terror. Shopkeepers inflated their prices for precious commodities like quinine and aspirin. Everywhere, people turned away in fear from strangers, from neighbors and friends, even from their own loved ones.

Yet heroism was also commonplace during the pandemic. Emergency hospitals were set up on private property donated by business owners, hotel and club managers, and fraternity houses. A makeshift hospital was erected in the Vanderbilt mansion in Rhode Island. Ambulances in the form of private cars, taxicabs, and the chauffeur-driven limousines of high society were also donated. Department stores distributed relief supplies and offered free use of their phones for emergency calls.

Off-duty policemen and firemen volunteered on ambulances and assisted medical personnel in hospitals. Teachers were recruited to work as home-duty nurses. Doctors and nurses worked night and day, treating the sick, handing out food, even milking cows, building fires, and cooking for families too ill to tend to their homes and farms. As historian A. A. Hoehling explained in his book about the Spanish influenza, *The Great Epidemic*, "There were two principal categories of people: those afflicted with the disease and those who endeavored to save them."

Elizabeth J. Davies, a nurse in Washington State, reported on the struggles of a family in her district:

> In one family a married daughter from Montana came to visit her [mother's] home, bringing with her a three-year-old child. The mother contracted influenza, infecting her daughter, who during the attack gave birth to a boy; the young husband arrived and came down at once with the disease; each developed pneumonia; a sister came to nurse them and she developed influenza in a few hours; another sister was telegraphed for and arrived on the scene with her family of two children, and all came down [with the flu]; there were not enough beds to accommodate the sick.

Ruth McKay, a 19-year-old clerk for the War Department, served as a volunteer during the pandemic.

When she finished work at 4 P.M. each day, she then walked to a nearby 500-bed emergency hospital in downtown Washington, D.C., where she tended to flu patients until ten o'clock at night. Her fiancé, a young grocer, picked up the tired girl in his Model T every night, disappointed that she was always too exhausted to venture out with him. "This is one hell of a romance!" he would complain as he drove Ruth home.

In the United States, the number of flu cases diminished during the latter part of November 1918 and never again reached the heights recorded in mid-autumn. But the number of new flu cases began to rise again in December, peaking by the end of January 1919. In New York City alone, more than 2,000 people died from Spanish influenza during the last month of 1918, and 1,000 New Yorkers perished in the last week of January 1919.

Once again, World War I eclipsed the Spanish influenza as the exciting news reports from the Paris Peace Conference commanded the front pages of newspapers and much of the newsreels. The third wave of the pandemic received very little attention, and many of the afflicted attributed their illness to a winter cold. In Paris, almost 3,000 people died from the flu during the months of December and January. Charles Seymour, the future president of Yale University, wrote home that "everyone has a cold here, and the Paris cold seems to take it out of one more than any I have known. I am all right now and quite chipper, but yesterday I felt as shaky as if I had had typhoid."

President Wilson, who at the time was the most popular man in the world, fell ill during the Paris Peace Conference with a convulsive cough, fever of

103°, and difficulty breathing. The onset of the disease was so abrupt that Wilson's personal physician at first suspected poisoning. The president's life was in danger during the first 12 hours, but he pulled through. His doctor's diagnosis was influenza.

President Wilson recovered from his severe case of Spanish flu, negotiating the Treaty of Versailles, the World War I peace treaty, from his sickroom. However, some historians believe that the flu permanently weakened the president—physically, emotionally, and mentally—and he began to act somewhat strangely following his recovery. Edmund W. Starling, the president's Secret Service guard, reported that "he never did regain his physical strength, and his weakness of body naturally reacted upon his mind. He lacked his old quickness of grasp." Starling repeatedly had to retrieve a briefcase full of secret documents that the president kept leaving behind.

Wilson's personal physician felt that the influenza was one of the factors that contributed to the president's eventual downfall. In September of 1919, President Wilson suffered a major stroke, which forced him to retire from public activity and disabled him for the remainder of his life.

By the time the Treaty of Versailles was signed on June 28, 1919, the Spanish influenza was a distant memory. Despite the best intentions included in the treaty's Covenant of the League of Nations, which was created specifically to prevent any more wars from occurring, World War II proved to be inevitable. The Spanish Lady, however, disappeared from the face of the earth she had so readily conquered. And the Spanish influenza has never returned—at least, not yet.

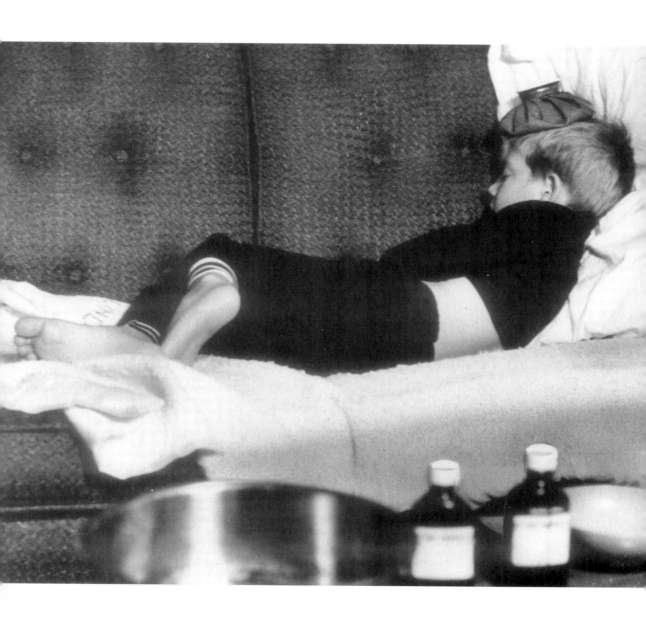

The flu—as much a part of winter as cold weather and holiday vacations. Because most strains of the influenza virus are relatively mild, few people think about the possibility of another deadly pandemic.

Killer Viruses Then and Now

D uring the pandemic of 1918, Philadelphia fared the worst of any major American city. In spite of the fact that the city's Bureau of Health had issued a bulletin in the summer of 1918 to warn residents about the Spanish influenza epidemic in Europe and its possible spread to America, Philadelphia did little to prepare for the onslaught that would soon occur. City health officials even failed to declare influenza a reportable disease until hundreds of flu-stricken sailors had been hospitalized inside the city limits.

The director of the Department of Health and Charities, Wilmer Krusen, informed Philadelphians that there was little chance the influenza would spread from enlisted men to civilians. Lieutenant

Commander R. W. Plummer, the medical aide to the commandant of the local naval district, announced publicly that the navy and city officials would "confine this disease to its present limits, and in this we are sure to be successful." The *Philadelphia Inquirer* reassured readers that the director of the medical research laboratories of the Phipps Institute of Philadelphia, Dr. Paul A. Lewis, had isolated the cause of Spanish influenza: Pfeiffer's bacillus. The discovery, claimed the widely read news report, "armed the medical profession with absolute knowledge on which to base its campaign against the disease."

Lulled by such false reassurances, the residents of Philadelphia continued to behave as if no threat to the public health existed. On September 28, 1918, approximately 200,000 Philadelphians gathered to watch the massive Liberty Loan parade, which stretched throughout the streets of the city.

In the days that immediately followed the parade, the Spanish influenza pandemic virtually exploded in the city of Philadelphia. By the middle of October, when more than 2,600 residents died one week and more than 4,500 the next, Philadelphia was in a state of extreme crisis.

Essential services were failing throughout the city. Hundreds of thousands of sick people overflowed the regular hospitals and flocked to the emergency flu hospitals that had been opened in state armories and churches. At the peak of the crisis, 487 police officers were too sick to go on duty. The Bureau of Child Hygiene was overrun with hundreds of children whose parents were ill, dying, or dead. And the city morgue, with a capacity of 36 bodies, was buried in

corpses. Piled three and four deep up and down the halls and in nearly every room, the hundreds of unembalmed, un-iced bodies were covered only with dirty, bloodstained sheets. The doors at the rear of the building had to be left open to vent some of the horrifying stench. So many bodies still remained in houses and apartments across the city that the city government had to take over a building that housed a cold storage plant

President Wilson at the head of a parade. The parades and large gatherings marking the end of the "war to end all wars" set the stage for another deadly round of influenza.

to use as a supplementary morgue. Before the pandemic ended, Philadelphia had enlisted the use of five supplementary morgues.

There were also shortages of coffins, embalmers, and grave diggers. Undertakers became the most despised people in the city when they stopped extending credit to poor families. Some private undertaking businesses increased their prices by as much as 600 percent. Cemetery owners charged burial fees, then forced the bereaved to dig the graves themselves.

The Philadelphia Council of National Defense finally stepped in to secure a guarantee of public funds for burying the poor. A convoy of six horse-drawn wagons and one truck drove about the city retrieving bodies that had been dead for up to four days. Volunteers collected a total of 221 corpses. Some of the bodies had been lowered from balconies by rope; others were discovered strewn about homes in which every single family member had died.

In just over a month—from September 29 to November 2, 1918—an estimated 12,162 Philadelphians died from the Spanish influenza. The citywide ordinance closing movie theaters, saloons, and hotels ended up costing well over $2 million in lost revenue. By Armistice Day, the Spanish influenza had cost the city of Philadelphia an estimated $60 million in deaths.

Of course, it was impossible then—as it is now—to put a price on the suffering and grief of families who lost loved ones to the Spanish Lady in Philadelphia, or in Boston and San Francisco, rural New Hampshire and the deep woods of Michigan, the bleak tundra of Alaska and the breezy islands of Samoa. After the Spanish Lady had completed her dance of death, the entire world was shrouded in grief.

Philadelphia was a typical city during the pandemic of 1918. City officials denied the true threat until it was irrefutable, permitted large war-related public gatherings, failed to report early incidences of the flu, and were unable to keep up city services during the peak wave of the disease. Health officials all over the United States had adopted a "What? Me worry?" attitude toward the approaching influenza pandemic until it was too late to institute preventive measures.

In New York City, for example, the health officer announced that there was no real danger from the influx of flu-stricken soldiers to hospitals (and saloons and rooming houses) all over the city in the early fall of 1918. In Baltimore, the health officer stated flatly, "There is no special reason I know of to fear an outbreak of disease in our city." The Chicago health officer reassured the city that "we have the Spanish Influenza situation well in hand now." All of these cities would be devastated by the second wave of the killer flu pandemic.

In 1918, public health officials were not well informed about the inevitability of public danger posed by the Spanish influenza pandemic. Medical authorities and political leaders were equally misinformed about the potential threat and the best methods for reducing the devastation. The opinion expressed by the *Journal of the American Medical Association* at the end of September 1918 was that Spanish influenza might be a new and unfamiliar name for the common flu, but that this fact "should not cause any greater importance to be attached to it, nor arouse any greater fear than would influenza without a new name." The public health authorities were, in fact, dead wrong.

In many cities, huge parades were staged even in the midst of the flu crisis in order to rev up public sentiment for the war and stimulate patriotic citizens to purchase war bonds. On October 12, 1918, President Wilson led a wildly enthusiastic throng of 25,000 patriots down the Avenue of the Allies, a street in New York City named to honor the nations allied in their opposition to Germany and Austria-Hungary. Only a few short weeks later, the Spanish influenza peaked in New York.

In 1918, there was no federal law requiring medical professionals to report cases of influenza. As the pandemic worsened, many cities instituted ordinances requiring such essential record keeping. But many cases of the Spanish influenza were never reported or recorded. At the time, no one could guess just how widespread, costly, and deadly the disease would prove to be.

If it had not been for the selfless sacrifices made by countless volunteers, cities hit hard by the 1918 influenza would have collapsed under the rotting piles of their own dead. In Philadelphia, for example, emergency hospitals, soup kitchens, and volunteer nurse and ambulance services abounded.

Volunteer work was dangerous, of course, because influenza was highly contagious, and the workday could last as long as 20 hours. Student nurses were assuming duties for which they would not be properly prepared for years. Medical students left their lecture halls for the flu hospitals, assuming the responsibilities of fully trained physicians. In this regard, the untrained volunteers sometimes proved to be a danger to the ill people they so generously tended. But for most people

suffering from the deadly flu, a helpful pair of hands was better than no assistance at all.

The women of Philadelphia, as in most every city and town in America, constituted the bulk of the non-professional volunteers, serving as amateur nurses, staff for soup kitchens, phone operators, ambulance drivers, and home helpers who would cook, clean, and close the eyes of the dead. Without a public health organization to oversee and assign volunteers, those who wanted to help simply walked out their own front doors and looked for people in need of assistance. In cities like Philadelphia, volunteers did not have to look

The heroic and selfless efforts of volunteers such as these members of the Women's Emergency Aid Corps helped alleviate the suffering caused by the influenza pandemic.

very hard to find work that desperately needed doing. Large advertisements appeared in the *Philadelphia Inquirer* that read: "Influenza Sufferers, If you need Physicians, Nurses, Ambulances, Motor Vehicles or any other service because of the epidemic, telephone 'Filbert 100' and when the number answers, say: Influenza." "Filbert 100" answered calls 24 hours a day. The telephone company quickly doubled, then quadrupled, the number of phone lines for the service.

Today, the Public Health Service (PHS) is a more highly organized, much better funded, and far more effective agency than the PHS of 1918. With a yearly budget of over $20 billion and more than 55,000 professional employees providing vital health services in every state, the PHS has succeeded in its primary mission of improving the nation's health and safety. PHS scientists, technicians, and administrators work together to monitor and control disease outbreaks and prevent the spread of infectious illnesses. The CDC in Atlanta and the National Institute of Allergy and Infectious Diseases near Washington, D.C., also work to keep infectious diseases like influenza epidemics under control.

In 1918, the surgeon general of the United States, Rupert O. Blue, had only a handful of doctors and researchers to assist him. His annual budget was less than $3 million. Flu was not a reportable disease, and many states failed to file death statistics of any kind with the federal government. The surgeon general's office not only lacked the funding to organize an effective preventive effort in 1918, it also lacked the necessary medical data. So even if the government had allocated the required funds for a nationwide

effort to forestall the pandemic, the short-staffed PHS would not have known what to do. At the time, no one knew what was best to do.

The unenlightened sanitation practices common in 1918 contributed to the spread of the Spanish influenza. Restaurants regularly scraped leftover meat from their customers' plates into simmering soup stocks. Food was stored in filthy, germ-ridden iceboxes. Few understood the importance of washing hands. In buildings that lacked plumbing, sewage was sometimes heaved into nearby alleys.

These days, such dangerously unsanitary practices are prevented by public health laws. Restaurants must

A nearly empty class-room attests to the broad reach of the Asian flu. The second serious influenza pandemic of the 20th century, the Asian flu claimed about 70,000 American lives in 1957—a death toll that, while sobering, pales in comparison with that of the Spanish influenza pandemic four decades earlier.

follow specific sanitation codes, and employees are routinely trained in healthful sanitation techniques. Raw sewage must be disposed of properly, and because of widespread public health education, most people understand the basics of preventing food-borne illnesses and the importance of keeping the spread of germs to a minimum.

The Spanish influenza of 1918 resulted in an expansion of the U.S. Public Health Service and spurred the development of what is widely regarded today as an unparalleled national system of reporting illnesses and deaths. Since 1918, the PHS has pioneered regulation to ensure the safety of the nation's food supply and all available medications; conducted ongoing surveillance of infectious diseases, including influenza; provided financial assistance for hospitals, medical schools, and states in need; developed sanitation programs to bring clean water and sewage disposal to tens of thousands of people; and delivered high-quality health care wherever needed.

In the years that followed the devastation of the Spanish flu pandemic, American public health policy improved significantly, and a vastly superior state of overall public health has resulted. The Spanish Lady succeeded in teaching America a number of important lessons that have proved essential to the maintenance of a healthy population.

At the same time, the worldwide devastation created by the most lethal influenza pandemic in history demonstrated all too clearly modern civilization's helplessness in the face of a great natural disaster. Most people who lived through the horror chose to quickly put the terrifying memories out of mind. For the scientific research community and the medical profession, however, the Spanish influenza of 1918 has continued to serve as a nagging reminder of a question as yet unanswered: Could a similar disaster be *prevented* in the future?

Today many laypersons are supremely confident that science could head off a public health disaster like the Spanish flu pandemic. Interestingly, however, many scientists don't share this optimistic outlook. "We've had a couple of generations of great fortune: since the . . . flu epidemic of 1918, there has not been a [lethal] pandemic disease that struck the human population," paleontologist and evolutionary biologist Stephen Jay Gould remarked during a lecture. "If you look through human history, a pandemic is everyday biology. With our usual hubris we felt that we'd learned through technological advances to be free of it forever. But we're not."

An estimated *2 billion* people were stricken with the Spanish influenza during the 10 ghastly months of the pandemic. Between 20 million and 40 million died in this short span, making the 1918 flu the most extensive and fastest-spreading killer disease in history. In the decades that have followed, scientists have uncovered the cause of the deadly flu, yet influenza continues to afflict the world's population. In fact, influenza may be the most dangerous infectious disease known to humankind.

Dr. Peter Palese, a genetic researcher and chairman of the Department of Microbiology at the Mount Sinai School of Medicine, makes the current-day threat posed by influenza frighteningly clear: "I always remind AIDS researchers," Palese says, "that many more people

A lab technician prepares swine flu samples for analysis, an early step in the production of a vaccine. In 1976, after a 19-year-old soldier died from the severe swine flu strain, health officials and pharmaceutical companies raced to produce millions of doses of vaccine, anticipating a pandemic like the one in 1918. The expected pandemic never materialized, however.

die of flu than AIDS. Between twenty thousand and fifty thousand die of flu in the U.S. every year, and even more in pandemic years. Flu is not so dramatic a disease, but clearly in terms of numbers over the years, AIDS is peanuts." (An estimated 38,780 AIDS-related deaths occurred in the United States in 1996.)

In 1918, the medical and scientific communities incorrectly blamed the deadly pandemic on the bacterium Pfeiffer's bacillus. But by 1933, the true cause of the Spanish influenza was isolated and identified: flu is a viral disease. In the years following this medical breakthrough, much more was learned about the influenza virus, including the fact that three types exist: type A, which causes most flu epidemics; type B, which causes relatively few cases but is associated with Reye's syndrome, a fatal illness in children; and type C, which appears not to cause any illness in humans at all.

According to contemporary viral researchers, the type-A flu virus is an excellent virus for study, a model for researching all other viruses. This is because the influenza virus continually changes itself so that the body's defense system cannot recognize it and build up immunity. The virus makes its self-changes as a matter of course, and our bodies simply cannot keep up. As a result, a new flu outbreak occurs every few years, and influenza vaccines become obsolete almost before they are used. Vaccines must be continually modified in order to keep up with the alterations constantly being made by the influenza virus. "I'm convinced that we'll never control flu virus by vaccination because the virus is too smart," predicts Dr. Robert Krug, chairman of the Department of Molecular Biology and Biochemistry at Rutgers University.

This pattern of continual self-change adopted by the influenza virus is termed "antigenic drift." The tricky flu virus also undergoes sporadic, far more dramatic changes, termed "antigenic shifts." With these shifts, the flu virus changes itself *completely* on a genetic level. This results in an all-new virus that invades with a vengeance, a virus with the potential to trigger a widespread and severe pandemic—such as the Spanish flu of 1918.

It is now possible for scientists to track these dangerous mutations of the influenza virus, but it is impossible to predict them. So despite decades of research, including years spent carefully tracking the drifts and shifts made by the influenza virus, as well as the development of flu vaccines and anti-influenza drugs, this crafty little microorganism continues to threaten the human population. The influenza virus still sickens people all over the globe—and one day, returning as a lethal influenza pandemic, it could massacre millions, just as it did in 1918.

Strains of influenza that proved lethal in strength and global in range have occurred only three times in the 20th century: in 1918; in 1957, when a new influenza strain, called the Asian flu, emerged; and again in 1968, when a third deadly strain, dubbed the Hong Kong flu, developed. The two more recent flu outbreaks were extremely mild, however, when compared with the Spanish influenza: the Asian flu killed around 70,000 Americans, and the Hong Kong flu proved deadly for some 28,000 people in the United States. This limited impact was attributed to the fact that most people had developed at least a partial immunity to the third (Hong Kong) strain, which turned out to be not too different in genetic structure from the second (Asian) strain.

In February of 1976, influenza experts believed that a deadly pandemic was on its way when a severe strain of the flu infected some young soldiers stationed at Fort Dix in New Jersey. One of the military recruits, 19-year-old Private David Lewis, died from the influenza virus. Research seemed to indicate that Lewis and four other victims had been infected with the same virus that had been responsible for the 1918 pandemic.

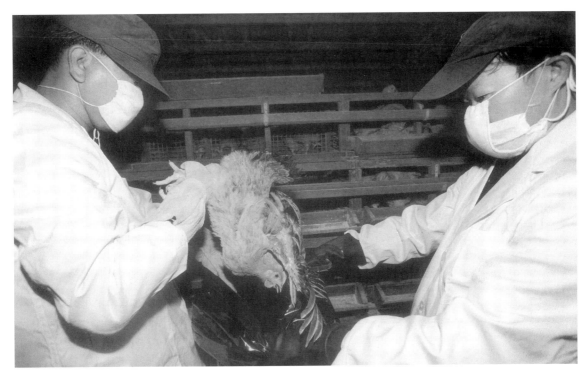

Public health officials immediately geared up for a repeat attack by the deadly Spanish influenza. This time, however, the authorities believed that they could head off the killer flu with vaccines, and thereby successfully prevent another global influenza disaster.

At the time, scientists had yet to uncover the genetic blueprint for the 1918 flu virus. Dr. Johan Hultin was busy practicing as a pathologist, his goal of tracking down live Spanish influenza virus still just a dream. It would be more than 20 years before Dr. Hultin would send to Dr. Jeffrey Taubenberger the infected lung tissue required to solve the genetic puzzle of the Spanish influenza virus.

But determined research scientists put together a vaccine anyway, one they believed could help recipients ward off the threatening influenza of 1976, which had

More than a million chickens were destroyed in Hong Kong in 1997, after the deaths of several farmers from a new "bird flu" strain. Today scientists know that deadly influenza strains can jump from chickens, ducks, or pigs to humans, and many such strains originate in regions of China where people live in close proximity to these animals.

been named the swine flu. Millions of doses of the high-quality vaccine—enough swine flu vaccine to protect every citizen of the United States—were manufactured and distributed. The large-scale effort proceeded smoothly within a matter of three or four months, an incredible public health achievement.

But the swine flu pandemic never materialized.

More than 40 million Americans received the swine flu vaccination in 1976. In retrospect, many experts now claim that these individuals were vaccinated for nothing—as there was no illness to be vaccinated against. In fact, the only real illness to emerge during the full-scale vaccination effort was actually caused by the vaccine: around 1,000 people developed a progressive paralysis, a disease called Guillain-Barré syndrome, which was traced directly to the response of their individual immune systems to the swine flu vaccine.

Still, the government and the scientific research community believed that they had acted prudently in attempting to avert another disaster like the pandemic of 1918. As Edwin Kilbourne, a public advocate of mass immunizations, has reminded those critical of the premature vaccinations of 1976: "Better a vaccine without an epidemic, than an epidemic without a vaccine."

Scientists now know that the development of a new, stronger viral strain in a few individuals does not necessarily signal the start of a pandemic. The swine flu simply died out on its own after infecting a small group of unlucky victims. In an article entitled "Swine Flu: The Virus that Vanished," Kilbourne wrote, "Early detection of a new virus therefore may not be adequate evidence on which to undertake mass immunization. But it is, I believe, a signal at least to produce vaccine to hold in readiness."

High-tech medical research and development firms have long attempted to create adjunct drugs for use in addition to influenza vaccines. Anti-influenza drugs that can be taken by mouth or in nasal sprays have been developed, but these medications are not regarded as being completely effective. In 1998, a do-it-yourself influenza diagnosis test kit was invented. The home test enables users to detect within 15 minutes whether or not their symptoms are actually due to influenza virus.

The ultimate development in the area of influenza virology, however, would be a universal vaccine effective against a wide range of strains. Such a vaccine could overcome the problems caused by "drift and shift" in the ever-changing influenza virus. Although such a universal vaccine remains a researcher's fantasy, a vaccine effective against the Spanish influenza or one of its descendant strains is now a reality.

The swine flu experience demonstrated that scientists have developed the technology, and the Public Health Service has created the organizational structure, required for a successful large-scale vaccination effort. And, with the recent discovery of its genetic blueprint by Dr. Jeffrey Taubenberger's team at the AFIP, the virus that made the Spanish Lady a worldwide killer *could*—if it ever reappeared—be conquered. But *would* it?

Although he is elated that he was able to contribute to the development of a vaccine to prevent another devastating Spanish influenza pandemic, Dr. Johan Hultin believes that the challenge facing scientists is far from over. In fact, Dr. Hultin points out, a whole new set of

A scene from the motion picture *12 · Monkeys*, which depicts a futuristic world in which a virus has killed billions of people and forced humanity underground. While the 1995 movie—like other recent Hollywood offerings about disease outbreaks—contains a fair dose of the improbable, not all is pure fantasy: experts say that another great pandemic is just a matter of time.

issues has now been raised. For example, if another deadly flu pandemic occurred, would the price of a vaccine be too high for much of the unindustrialized world? If the flu shot cost two or three dollars per person, would the wealthier nations be willing to spend $15 billion or more to help everyone receive a vaccine? And in this era of jet travel, which could spread a flu virus throughout the world in only a few *weeks*, would the several *months* it takes to manufacture and distribute a vaccine actually be enough time?

"Should the need arise," Dr. Hultin states, "a vaccine *must* be made available to the extent of what is possible economically, logistically, and politically." Whether or not the necessary vaccine can be created and distributed globally in time to prevent another worldwide disaster like the pandemic of 1918 remains a big unknown.

In financial circles it is said that "when Hong Kong sneezes, the world catches cold"—an allusion to the significant impact the tiny Chinese-controlled territory has on the world's financial markets. But the saying is also quite applicable to the incidence of influenza pandemics. Researchers now believe that the 1918 Spanish influenza actually originated in China—as did the Asian flu and the Hong Kong flu.

Influenza experts have discovered that the three most recent global flu pandemics got their start on the farms of southern China, where ducks live in close quarters with pigs and people. It is now known that the flu virus came from wild ducks, which spread the disease to pigs, which in turn passed it on to the farm families who tended them. During the transmission from animals to humans, the influenza virus underwent a major antigenic shift, resulting all three times in a totally new killer flu.

The world's scientific researchers are watching southern China carefully, especially since the recent emergence of a few isolated cases of "bird flu," in which Chinese people living in rural areas appear to have contracted influenza from chickens. This particular strain of the flu virus seems to be inefficiently transmitted, so most people who have contact with infected chickens remain healthy. Just in case, however, a bird flu vaccine was prepared in 1997.

For years, the scientific community has been getting ready for what it sees as the inevitable next flu pandemic. In 1978, the CDC drafted its first plan for resolving the major technical, political, and administrative issues that proved so problematic in 1918, 1957, 1968, and again in 1976. In 1993, the Federal Working Group on Influenza was formed, and these influenza experts updated the CDC plan and implemented it as public policy.

That same year, representatives from 13 European countries met to draft their own plan for dealing with the next influenza pandemic. Two years later, an international coalition of government agencies and private associations devised a global blueprint for controlling any future flu pandemics. To watch out for emerging new strains of the influenza virus, the 1995 plan called for increased monitoring in China.

Even though the international research and policy group agreed on the general principles for dealing with a global influenza outbreak and affirmed that such a worldwide effort could indeed prove successful, the details regarding the appropriation of the funds required to mount such a massive effort were never established. Walter Dowdle, Ph.D., informed the international assembly, "If we expect to have an impact on the next pandemic it will take money. It's going to cost. But the cost of pandemic preparedness will be negligible compared with the cost of an inappropriate or inadequate response."

Kennedy F. Shortridge, Ph.D., professor of microbiology at the University of Hong Kong, believes that the next pandemic of killer influenza will soon emerge from China—or possibly Southeast Asia or some other location where people and animals live in close proximity. "We're not going to stop the pandemic, but we have to get ahead of the virus in time to get it to manufacturers for vaccine production," Dr. Shortridge warns. "It's a massive task, and unless we get cracking on it right away, we're liable to miss the boat."

If Dr. Johan V. Hultin and the other influenza experts are accurate in their predictions, there *will* be another pandemic of killer influenza virus. And when the next flu disaster strikes—very possibly within the next few years—all of us may have the opportunity to test our immune systems, our survival skills, and our potential for heroism.

Chronology

1847–48 First influenza pandemic strikes; is mild in U.S.

1889 Second influenza pandemic, nicknamed "Chinese distemper," strikes; once again, is mild in U.S.

1914 World War I begins

1917 United States declares war against Germany

1918 *March:* First recorded case of Spanish influenza, at Fort Riley, Kansas; first wave of pandemic begins

May: Soldiers carry influenza to France; Royal Navy brings flu back to England

June: Influenza spreads through Germany, Austria-Hungary, Switzerland; crosses Pacific Ocean to infect Hawaii

July: Spanish influenza sweeps Spain, Norway, China, Japan, Sierra Leone, Russia, Alaska, elsewhere

August: Influenza spreads throughout U.S. port cities, including New York, Boston, New Orleans, Seattle; second wave begins

September: Spanish influenza attacks soldier training camps and begins infecting civilians across U.S.

October: India reports 5 million dead; influenza reports arrive from islands of South Pacific and other far outposts of civilization

Early November: Spanish influenza begins to recede in U.S., continues to kill in Europe, elsewhere

November 11: Armistice Day; World War I officially ends

Late November: Spanish influenza fades out in Europe

December: Third wave of Spanish influenza begins

1919 Third wave of Spanish influenza peaks in U.S. in January; by spring Spanish influenza dies out across globe

1930s Influenza virus isolated and identified with development of electron microscope

Chronology

1957   Asian flu kills 98,000 worldwide

1968   Hong Kong flu wipes out 46,000 across globe

1976   Swine flu immunization—without expected outbreak

1993   Federal Working Group on Influenza forms, implements global plan for controlling future influenza pandemic(s)

1997   Johan Hultin digs up Lucy, sends lung tissue to Armed Forces Institute of Pathology (AFIP)

1998   Researchers at AFIP identify genetic code for Spanish influenza, making development of vaccine possible

Further Reading

Crosby, Alfred W. *America's Forgotten Pandemic: The Influenza of 1918*. New York: Cambridge University Press, 1989.

Fincher, Jack. "America's Deadly Rendezvous with the 'Spanish Lady.'" *Smithsonian*, January 1989, pp. 131–145.

Foreman, Michael. *War Game*. New York: Arcade, 1993.

Frost, Bob. "Conquering a Killer Virus." *Biography Magazine*, October 1998, pp. 82–86.

Garrett, Laurie. *The Coming Plague: Newly Emerging Diseases in a World Out of Balance*. New York: Farrar, Straus and Giroux, 1994.

Gay, Kathlyn, and Martin Gay. *World War I*. New York: Twenty First Century Books, 1995.

Gladwell, Malcolm. "The Dead Zone." *The New Yorker*, September 29, 1997, pp. 52–65.

Henig, Robin Marantz. "Flu Pandemic: Once and Future Menace." *The New York Times Magazine*, November 29, 1992, p. 28.

Hoehling, A. A. *The Great Epidemic*. Boston: Little, Brown and Company, 1961.

Kolata, Gina B. *Flu: The Story of the Great Influenza Pandemic of 1918 and the Search for the Virus that Caused It*. New York: Farrar, Straus and Giroux, 1999.

Lampton, Christopher. *Epidemic*. Brookfield, Conn.: The Millbrook Press, 1992.

Levine, Arnold J. *Viruses*. New York: Scientific American Library, 1992.

Porter, Katherine Ann. *Pale Horse, Pale Rider*. New York: Random House, 1936.

Roden, Katie. *Plague*. Brookfield, Conn.: Copper Beech Books, 1996.

Stewart, Gail. *World War I*. San Diego, Calif.: Lucent Books, 1991.

Index

VIRGINIA ARONSON is a health writer and author of more than a dozen books on nutrition, fitness, and healthy living. She has also written several titles for Chelsea House, including *How to Say No* in the JUNIOR DRUG AWARENESS series. Ms. Aronson lives in South Florida with her writer husband and their young son.

JILL McCAFFREY has served for four years as national chairman of the Armed Forces Emergency Services of the American Red Cross. Ms. McCaffrey also serves on the board of directors for Knollwood—the Army Distaff Hall. The former Jill Ann Faulkner, a Massachusetts native, is the wife of Barry R. McCaffrey, a member of President Bill Clinton's cabinet and director of the White House Office of National Drug Control Policy. The McCaffreys are the parents of three grown children: Sean, a major in the U.S. Army; Tara, an intensive care nurse and captain in the National Guard; and Amy, a seventh grade teacher. The McCaffreys also have two grandchildren, Michael and Jack.

Picture Credits